Contemporary Spirituality: Responding to the Divine Initiative

Contemporary Spirituality: Responding to the Divine Initiative

Francis A. Eigo, O.S.A.
Editor

The Villanova University Press

Copyright© 1983 by Francis A. Eigo, O.S.A.
The Villanova University Press
Villanova, Pennsylvania 19085
All rights reserved
Library of Congress Cataloging in Publication Data
Main entry under title:
Contemporary spirituality, responding to the divine
  initiative.

  Includes index.
  1. Spiritual life—Addresses, essays, lectures.
I. Eigo, Francis A.
BV4501.2.C6725   1983   248.4   83-1166
ISBN 0-87723-037-4

To

the

Memory

of

Joseph Papin

Contents

Contributors

WILLIAM R. CALLAHAN, S.J., Codirector of the Quixote Center, has authored or edited several books, including *The Quest for Justice, The Wind is Rising,* and *Look! A New Thing on the Americas.*

DORIS DONNELLY, professor at Princeton Theological Seminary, consultant on adult education for the Diocese of Trenton, president of the Ecumenical Institute of Spirituality, lectures widely and is the author of numerous articles and such books as *Learning to Forgive, Putting Forgiveness into Practice,* and *Coming Closer: Stages in the Spiritual Journey.*

MICHAEL FISHBANE, professor of Biblical Studies at Brandeis University, has published widely, in both English and Hebrew, in the areas of Biblical Studies and the Dead Sea Scrolls, and is the author of *Text and Texture: Close Readings of Selected Biblical Texts.*

RICHARD McSORLEY, S.J., Director of the Center for Peace Studies at Georgetown University and a professor of theology there, is the author of many articles and several books, including *Kill? for Peace?, Peace Eyes, The New Testament Basis of Peacemaking,* and *The More the Merrier.*

JOHN SHEA, consultant, lecturer, professor at Saint Mary of the Lake Seminary, has authored numerous articles and numbers among his books *The Challenge of Jesus, The Hour of the Unexpected, Stories of God, Stories of Faith,* and the forthcoming *Religious Language in a Secular Culture* and *Story and Doctrine.*

JULIA UPTON, professor of theology at Saint John's University (Jamaica, Long Island), is an advisor to the Bishops' Committee on the Liturgy, a consultant to the International Commission on English in the Liturgy, as well as the author of a number of articles.

Introduction

This fifteenth volume of the *Proceedings of the Theology Institute of Villanova University* contains essays which examine various ways of responding to the Divine Initiative: the Jewish response (Michael Fishbane's essay), Jesus' Response (John Shea's essay), some Christian Responses (Doris Donnelly's essay on Prayer, Richard McSorley's on Peace and Justice, Julia Upton's on Liturgy/Eucharist/World, and William Callahan's on the evolving vision of the Great Commandment).

I wish to take this occasion to thank those who have contributed to the Theology Institute and to this volume of the *Proceedings:* John M. Driscoll, O.S.A., James J. Cleary, Emily Binns, Arthur Crabtree, Bernard Lazor, O.S.A., Bernard Prusak, Patricia Fry, and the essayists — William Callahan, Doris Donnelly, Michael Fishbane, Richard McSorley, John Shea, Julia Upton.

Francis A. Eigo, O.S.A.
Editor

Jewish Perspectives on Prayer and Living

Michael Fishbane

It would certainly be a vain attempt, and one entirely out of keeping with the objectives of this Theology Institute, to try to set before you anything like a comprehensive view of the content and range of Jewish prayer. For one thing, Jewish prayer, quite apart from its vast and influential biblical patrimony, is an outpouring of over two thousand years, with prayers ranging over the detailed minutiae of everyday life and special sacred moments, and reflecting the life of the many Jewish communities in all the lands of its dispersion. And so, to try to describe this vast corpus, in this or almost any other framework, would be foolhardy indeed. Moreover, as noted, such a pursuit would also be inappropriate for this conference, which is at once selective in its focus on theological components of Jewish prayer, and concerned to relate Jewish prayer to the life of Jewish piety more broadly—both from an historical perspective and, I assume, from a contemporary one as well. It is with these issues in mind that I shall address you on some "Jewish Perspectives on Prayer and Living." My procedure—which I wish you to have in mind from the outset—will be, first, to treat the phenomenon of prayer in traditional Judaism from the perspective of several major religious principles or presuppositions embedded within it; then, second, to consider the biblical background of Jewish prayer, insofar as the prayers of the Hebrew Bible formed the conceptual underpinning of prayers within classical Judaism and provided the raw content of those prayers. In that discussion, I shall again not attempt a comprehensive description—for such surveys have often enough been done—but shall rather try to isolate several significant religious dynamics which are both part of the life experience of biblical prayer and formative of later "Jewish Perspectives." In the third section, I

1

shall return to the issue of Jewish prayer, and, with several brief and regrettably broad strokes, invert elements of the earlier discussions, so that you will see how diverse, theologically revolutionary, and even 'anti-biblical' Jewish prayer could be and was. And finally, in the fourth section, I shall speak to you as one modern Jew, and make some personal comments on Jewish prayer in my life of faith—set as it is within Judaism generally, modernity more broadly, and the religious consciousness of one twentieth-century American Jew, to speak even more narrowly and idiosyncratically.

I

At the very heart of Judaism, and its complex life and institutions, is its life of prayer. I use this phrase, 'life of prayer,' deliberately; not solely to indicate to you that in Judaism one can have a prayer life, that is, a dimension of the religious self which is in communion or relationship with God. This phenomenon is, of course, existent within Judaism, as will become fully evident in the course of my discussion. I rather say 'life of prayer' in order to stress that, in traditional Judaism, *one's prayer life is part and parcel of one's religious life;* it is an ongoing and inextricable part of one's Jewish being. As a member of a so-called positive religion, that is, a religion based on the content of divine revelation, itself variously defined and redefined through exegesis, the Jew has commandments, or *mitzvot,* to obey and to perform. These commandments, as is well known, encompass every detail of the Jew's daily life, and prescribe many positive actions—those which one must do—and many negative ones as well—those which one must not do. Thus, the Jew must "observe" the Sabbath, but must "not" work thereon; he "may" eat certain foods but may "not" eat others; he must "love" God and "honor" one's parents as fixed duties, but must "not kill" or "covet" or "steal"; and so on. Prayer in Judaism is also a positive religious duty, a *mitzvah aseh* in rabbinic terms; and though not all the normative aspects of proper prayer were derivable from Scripture, it nevertheless came about that the rules of prayer are a central and obligatory component of Judaism's *vita activa.* Prayer, then—at once paradoxically and characteristically enough for Judaism—is a commandment with many rules. Over time, the rules of prayer proliferated: one rabbinic generation added to another,[1] and gradually, by the Middle Ages, not only were fixed orders of prayer fixed, but the rules were summarized in the great legal compendia which came from the pen of Judaism's greatest sages—like the *Book of Love,* the *Sefer Ahabah,* of Maimonides' Code, the *Mishneh Torah;* or like the rules of prayer in Rabbi Joseph Karo's Code, the *Shulhan Arukh,* several centuries later (from the sixteenth century).

The life of prayer within Judaism thus covers the when, the how, and the what of a fixed religious duty. A Jew is required by rabbinic law to prayer three times daily, and also on Sabbaths, festivals and special fast days; and each of these services is long, complex and various. Indeed, the Jew begins his prayer life with his first breath and ends it with his last. At the very beginning of the day, and here I mean, literally, at the very beginning of daily consciousness, a prayer is recited which thanks God for restoring one's soul, in grace, and avers that the beginning of wisdom is the fear of the Lord, whose praise is everlasting. Thus, in terms of the title of this conference, "Responding to the Divine Initiative," such a response is immediate and daily in Jewish liturgy. Following these words, the Jew then proceeds to enunciate a detailed series of blessings which thank God for human knowledge and consciousness, for being a Jew and able to praise, for giving sight to the blind and raiment to the naked, and so on—all *before* the fixed order of prayer in the community even begins. Let me cite here selected aspects of these prayers, in order to give you a very brief glimpse of their content and concern:

> My God, the soul you have given me is pure. You created it and You formed it. You breathed it into me and You keep it within me . . .

> So long as the soul is within me I acknowledge You, O Lord my God and God of my fathers, Master of all creation, Lord of all souls. Praised are You, O Lord, who restores the soul to the body.

*

> Praised are You, O Lord our God, King of the universe, who enables man to distinguish between night and day.

> Praised are You, O Lord our God, King of the universe, who fashioned man in Your image.

> Praised are You, O Lord our God, King of the universe, who has placed upon me the responsibilities of a Jew.

> Praised are You, O Lord our God, King of the universe, who gives sight to the blind.

> Praised are You, O Lord our God, King of the universe, who created heaven and earth.

> Praised are You, O Lord our God, King of the universe, who provides for all my needs.[2]

The human being, the Jew, thus responds to the divine initiative of life itself, at the daily renewal of life, at the first moments of waking consciousness and creature consciousness: for it is at such moments that one is singularly aware of physical and spiritual lack and physical and spiritual dependency. The creature acknowledges that he neither initiates his own life, nor that of the world at large; he confirms, rather, that he is initiated, created by God—as is the world. What the human creature can, however, initiate, is prayer; and this, according to rabbinic Judaism, is his duty and obligation.

The divine initiative thus begins for the Jew with the creation. This act is an initial and initiatory act of grace—one that takes on different articulations through the revelation of the Torah and its teachings, and through the redemptions of past and future. Stress on the creation, and God as the creator, is thus central to the daily morning (as of other) liturgies:

> Praised are You, O Lord our God, King of the universe.
> You fix the cycles of light and darkness;
> You ordain the order of all creation.
> You cause light to shine over the earth;
> Your radiant mercy is upon its inhabitants.
>
> In Your goodness the work of creation
> Is continually renewed day by day.
>
> How manifold are Your works, O Lord!
> With wisdom you fashioned them all!
> The earth abounds with Your creations.[3]

In these words, the official rabbinic liturgy gives expression to its central belief that the divine initiative of the creation is a recurrent initiative; indeed, that it is an initiative renewed daily, even momentarily; and that the creation is, in itself, an expression of God's "radiant mercy." An interesting and spiritually profound reflex of these ideas is found outside the traditional liturgy, as well, from the *Wisdom of Solomon.* There, it is not only stated that the "radiant mercy" of God is set over the creation and its inhabitants, but that the creation is, *as such,* infused with this mercy—the very ground of its being, as it were:

> Thou has mercy on all,
> for thou canst do all things,
> and thou overlookest the sins of men
> because they should amend.
> For thou lovest all things that are,
> and abhorrest nothing which thou has made;
> for never would thou have made any thing if thou didst
>   hate it.
> And how could any thing have endured if it had not been
>   thy will?
> Or been preserved, if not called by thee?
> But thou sparest all:

> for they are thine,
> O Lord, thou lover of souls;
> for thine incorruptible spirit is in all things.[4]

In response to all this, the initiative of mankind is praise and thanksgiving. Religious consciousness is thus marked here as recognizing the self as part of the created universe, as a creation among creations; and, even more, as an expression of the very divine mercy and grace which sustain and renew life itself. Thus, one lives by, in, and through grace—taken concretely, as the creation itself; and one partakes of divine grace through breath and food, vision and wonder, building *and prayer*. Responding to the God-given bounty of this world, the great Tannaitic sage, Rabbi Meir, said, in the Talmud, that one should recite at least one hundred blessings a day. Thus, one may not suffice with reciting the many fixed blessings found in the prayer services; for the wonders of creation are ever present. Not to thank God for the world and its sustenance is, according to the early sages, to be a thief; for a thief takes what is not his, and appropriates it as his own.[5] To eat and not to give thanksgiving; to feel the rain and wind and not to bless the lord of creation; to enjoy smell and love and not to be grateful, is thievery. Human gratitude, which is nothing else, when addressed to God, than the return of grace, is the only proper human initiative in response to the divine one. And so, Judaism has authorized many prayers for all the events of life.

Responding to the divine initiative of creation and sustenance thus requires that the creature, the Jew, be constantly aware of his creature-hood and the creation, and articulate this awareness through prayers which aver God's *abiding presence*. Thus, for example, after each meal, the Jew initiates a response of thanksgiving, which begins:

> Blessed are You, O Lord our God, King of the universe, who in his goodness feeds the entire world, in grace, in mercy and in compassion. He gives food to all flesh, for his mercy is everlasting.

> And because of his great goodness, we have never lacked food—and may we never suffer for want of it.

> For his great Name's sake—for he feeds and provides for all—he does good to the world and bestows food for all his creatures.

> Blessed are You, O Lord,
> who feeds all living things.[6]

Even a modern Hebrew writer, particularly known for his rejection of traditional Judaism and his dark pessimism, prayed:

> My Father, Father of orphans,
> be gracious unto me,

send me the sun's rays as a gift.
And I, an orphan of orphans,
shall receive thy gift with thanks, with love, with hope.
I know how to prize thy gift, thy goodness, Selah!
My heart sings and shouts to thee,
O Father of life,
blessed art thou, Selah.[7]

*

But, it is not only Creation which is the gift of God for the Jew. The grace of creation is refocused as wisdom and guidance through Revelation, through the covenant and its teachings. This, too, is a divine initiative, a grace—"our life and the length of our days," as the liturgy expresses it. The God of Israel, proclaims the Jew, is not a god of grace and law; but One whose law *is* his grace, and whose grace *is* expressed through the law. In the words of the liturgy:

Deep is Your love for us, O Lord our God;
Bounteous is Your compassion and tenderness.
You taught our fathers the laws of life,
And they trusted in You, Father and King.

For their sake be gracious unto us, and teach us,
That we may learn Your laws and trust in You.
Father, merciful Father, have compassion upon us;
Endow us with discernment and understanding.

Grant the will to study Your Torah,
To heed its words and to teach its precepts.
May we observe and practice its instruction,
Lovingly fulfilling all its teachings.

Enlighten our eyes to Your Torah,
Open our hearts to Your commandments.
Unite our thoughts with singleness of purpose
To hold You in reverence and love.[8]

Here a note is struck that pervades the broadest reaches of the Jew's religious consciousness and life of prayer. The divine gift of Torah is an act of compassionate instruction, whose response is thankfulness by the Jew, who must complete this divine initiative with his own: In study, observance and devotion. Thus, the Jew rehearses the central values of Judaism in his prayer, and prepares to actualize this prayer in life, in the community. In prayer, the Jew confronts the fact that God is not only the source of life, but, further, the source of meaning, value, culture—even truth. In this way, prayer becomes a meditative articulation of the divinely sponsored teachings which constitute Judaism, and challenges the reciter to translate his life into a realization of his prayers.

So much is it the case that Torah and its contents are a primary divine initiative, responded to in prayer, that readings from the Torah (e.g., the binding of Isaac, Genesis 22; or the Song of the Sea, Exodus 15) are incorporated into the weekday service; that the weekly Torah lection is read at the climax of certain weekday services, and primarily Sabbath, with special readings for Holidays, and that fragments of citations from Scripture make up the fabric of a considerable amount of rabbinic prayer. This recitation from sections of the Pentateuch and the Psalter, as well as the Torah lections, in the course of the prayer service, strikingly demonstrates the extent to which Judaism is predicated on the divine initiative as expressed through the revealed law. Indeed, one may even regard the liturgical movement of the early part of a service in which the Torah is read publicly as a spiritual movement towards the center of faith; as an ever-renewed encounter with the God of Sinai and His teachings. And lest one think—and for a traditional Jew this would be impossible—that the written law is separable from the oral teachings which explain, extend and delimit it, the morning service includes rabbinic statements on the duty and value of Torah study, whose "fruits" are illimitable; blessings for Torah and its study (which traditionally has come to mean *all* rabbinic materials—though originally it meant only the Torah of Moses and the Mishnah); and a listing of the ancient hermeneutical rules of Rabbi Ishmael. So much is this material actually considered to be study, that a special sanctification prayer is recited which adds to the basic formulary (which extolls God for his majestic exaltation) a reference to the Rabbis and the teachers. How remarkable all this is should be readily apparent; for just think: here one's prayers *include* study of the Torah and rabbinic teachings—and these are, in living practice, *prayed* in just the same manner as prayers of thanksgiving, praise and petition.

A tenuous line is thus drawn between prayer and study—a line whose tenuousness is felt everywhere in Judaism. For, though there were some ancient sages who regretted the time spent in prayer, prayer was often conceived of as a more important act of piety and communion with God; this orientation was never endorsed. Rather, the two forms—prayer and study—have been generally regarded by traditional Judaism as *complementary* religious modalities which respond to the divine initiative. A later prayer, attributed to King David, preserved in the medieval collection of Midrash called the *Seder Eliyahu Rabba,* voices a related theme; namely, that the grace of the revelation of Torah is an initiative which opens the faithful Jew to the possibility of the world to come. Indeed, it initiates him on a course of beatitude and personal salvation.

> My Father who art in heaven,
> blessed be thy great name for all eternity

> and mayest thou find contentment from Israel, thy
>   servants, wherever they may dwell.
> Thou hast reared us, made us great, sanctified us,
>   praised us;
> thou hast bound on us the crown of the words of Torah,
> they that reach from one end of the world to the other.
> Whatever of Torah I have fulfilled, came only through thee;
> whatever loving-kindness I have shown, came only through thee;
> In return for the little Torah that I have done before thee
> thou has given me a share in this world, in the days of
>   the Messiah, and in the world to come.[9]

The grace of divine revelation thus opens the Jew, in prayer, to the majestic power of God that orders and redeems. The gift of Torah is thus a token of a more munificent divine fulfillment; a past event that bears the seeds of hope for those who walk in the ways of the Lord. But, future hope for the Jew, as it is theologically stressed and recited in prayer, builds on the memory of past acts of redemption; for such particular national events of divine grace as the exodus, which initiates freedom and responsibility for the Jew, constitute the shape of memory and the seeds of hope. Over and over in the liturgy, and in the festival cycle of ritual acts and prayers, the Jew recalls the exodus from Egypt. Through this recollection, he is reconfirmed in his waiting in hope for a remanifestation of divine grace—one that will redeem the Jews from their contemporary historical bondage and exile. Indeed, so strong is this theme of redemption that, for example, the prayer recited earlier, celebrating the renewal of God's acts of creation daily, closes with a prayer for a return of the light of creation to Zion; just as the aforenoted prayer, reciting the divine revelation and the grace of Torah and study, concludes with a prayer for the ingathering of the Jewish exile, in peace, from the four corners of the earth. Similarly, after the recitation of the unity of God, in the *Shema,* an even more forceful emphasis on redemption is sounded—in which the themes of God as Creator and Revealer are combined with the thematics of divine Redemption, and the old exodus is recalled as warrant for future hope. Thus, in the language of the old liturgy:

> You have been our fathers' protector of old,
> Shield for them and their children,
> Our Deliverer through all generations.
>
> Though You dwell in the highest heights,
> Your just decrees reach out everywhere.
> They extend to the very ends of the earth.
>
> Happy the man who obeys Your commandments,
> Who lays to heart the words of Your Torah.

You are, in truth, Lord of Your people,
You are their Defender and mighty King.

You are the first and You are the last;
We have no King or Redeemer but You.

You, O Lord our God, rescued us from Egypt;
You redeemed us from the house of bondage

. . . .

Then Your beloved sang hymns of thanksgiving;
They extolled You with psalms of adoration.

. . . .

The redeemed sang a new song for You;

. . . .

Acclaiming Your sovereignty with thanksgiving:

The Lord shall reign for ever and ever!

Rock of Israel, arise to Israel's defense!
Fulfill Your promise to deliver Judah and Israel.

Our Redeemer is the Holy One of Israel,
The Lord of hosts is His name.
Praised are You, O Lord, Redeemer of Israel.[10]

In these various words it becomes clear that memory is based on a divine initiative which is celebrated and reconfirmed daily in prayer. Memory is thus a vital part of the daily life of faith for the Jew; orienting him to the past; giving him a standpoint in the present; and opening him to a vision of hope and trust. Moreover, the recitation in the above prayer of past divine acts of redemptions reminds the Jew that the proper response to the divine initiative of redemption is a proclamation of His Lordship; an intonement of His praise; and an undiminished request for the final Redemption. In this way, prayer becomes the context for reaffirmations of theological truths, revealed through history; and a means of educating the Jew for collective hope. One prays first in the language of the ancients, recalling their praise and faith; and then, on this basis, one prays for the needs of the immediate hour. Though the Jew knows—historically and physically—that the final redemption is not yet, in its fulness, and that only tokens have been granted, he also experiences these tokens as sufficient to sustain hope, and to transform the fragments of existence into the secret ground from which the final planting will spring. For, in truth, the flower will be the blossom of an ancient seed; when the ancient divine initiative will fulfill the trust placed in it. Israel's response to the ancient initiative of redemption is to keep the memory of it alive, unwaveringly, in the darkness of history. Israel's initiative is thus a waiting in hope, a waiting in memory, a waiting with petition: in truth, a waiting which always resists guarantees and promises which are not ultimate. Israel resists the idolization of the Redemption to come: for the sake of past memory, for the sake of present hopes, and for the sake of God's Truth—no less.

*

In prayer, as we have seen, the Jew is thrown—throws himself— totally upon God, *upon the living God.* There is no room in such verbal prayer for abstract and theoretical notions: for the One who is addressed is the God of Abraham, Isaac and Jacob—not the god of the philosophers. God as Creator, Revealer and Redeemer initiates what no person can initiate: the love and grace of a supportable world; the love and grace of teachings for concrete life; and the love and grace of past salvations with their promise of a future. In all these respects the person is a receiver; is passive; is a respondent. But, it is singularly in prayer—though, of course, not only here—that the person can also respond to the divine initiative. For in prayer, the person can open himself to the supportable ground of his life, to the Teacher of his ways, and to the leading hand of God; indeed, in prayer the Jew is set over-against the Otherness of God, and is forcefully aware of his dependence upon the divine reality.

The creations of God flood by the person, and he responds with words of thanksgiving; the teachings of God addressed the person with *mitzvah* and task, and this is acknowledged; and earthly lack confronts one with human limitations, and so the needful soul addresses requests to God, the 'Breath of all Life,' and waits. Prayer thus initiates what is human and not godly; it initiates human thanksgiving and petition before the tremulous nature of existence. Prayer sets the mark of the creature who is not a creator; of a learner who is not a revealer; and of an actor who is not the fulfiller of all hopes. It sets the mark of the creature, because verbal prayer—such as that reviewed above—never permits the speaker to imagine his (even potential) divinity; nor does it ever allow the speaker to regard himself or his world as an abstraction. Insofar as God is addressed as a living God, as the God of the Universe, it is the concreteness of life and existence, given by God, which finds expression in Jewish prayer. Abstractions have no place.

Several of these points must be underscored—and this for two reasons: because of their inherent and pervasive importance in Judaism, as it developed from the Bible; and because—as we shall have occasion to observe in a later section—such notions do not exhaust the living Jewish attitude towards prayer. Thus, to repeat, what is particularly striking about aspects of Jewish prayer, as seen hitherto, is the absolute difference between man and God. Prayer does not try to overcome this difference; indeed, this difference is the very ground and framework of verbal prayer. Praise and petition only deepen the true difference between the creature and the creator; and, though they bring the two into relation, they underscore the vital distinction between human dependency and divine grace. Moreover, the basic presupposition of all earlier remarks is that the divine is attentive to the praying person; that God responds, hears, attends, sees, and so forth. This projection of attributes upwards towards the divine is rarely inhibited in the popular, traditional Jewish liturgy—where prayer is voiced by the collectivity of Israel in *quorum,* not by philosophers or apologists uncomfortable with Jewish prayer's anthropomorphisms and anthropopathisms. One might rather say that, most commonly in Judaism, the projection of human attributes upon God actually works to renew the immediacy and personal nature of prayer before God. It is the robing of God with the garments of personhood that underscores the unassimilable Otherness of the divine being; and sustains the tangible, living quality of divinity—as the soul and will of the world—before whom prayer is 'efficacious.'

Precisely what is involved in the efficacy of prayer varies, of course, throughout the millennia of Jewish prayer. At its core, however, and reiterated by the sages and masters of the Tradition, is the notion that God "hears prayer" (cf., in the great *Amidah* prayer, the appeal: "Hear our voice, O Lord, our God; have mercy and compassion for us!"). The religious teaching that God "hears" prayer means, quite broadly, that God is providentially attentive to the 'expressions' of creaturehood; that He is 'alive' to human need; and that He is 'inclined'—at some dimension of His being—towards the human surge that inclines toward God. And more: the 'hearing' of God also valorizes the speech of mankind in prayer. When the Jew says, or affirms, that God "hears prayer," he is theologically affirming the worth of his language and the value of his needs; and further, he is affirming that divinity, in its way and in its time, also *confirms* the worth of human language and the value of human needs. Thus, although the stress on the transcendence of God effectively tempered the magical aspects of prayer language in Judaism—i.e., the language of prayer was somehow independently efficacious, or capable of operating effectively upon God—the requirements of living prayer *expressed through words* inevitably meant that the aura of prayer's efficacy, which has ever and always charged the contents of verbal prayer, was never completely neutralized.

There are many ways that the preceding paragraph could be developed. In the interests of space, and our present concern, one particular aspect of this issue may be touched on through brief reflections on the notion of *kavvanah,* or attentiveness and concentration in the act of prayer. Certainly in the early stages of Judaism, no less than in later stages, the 'expectancy'—even 'expectant certainty'—that verbal prayers would be heard and answered by God was a basic presupposition. Nevertheless, a strong spiritualizing concern is articulated in our earliest rabbinic sources; where, for example, it is stressed that the worshipper must be conscious of the words he utters in prayer—for only in such a manner would they truly be directed (*kavven*) to Heaven. Thus, in the ancient Mishnah, it is reported that the "early Hasidim [pietists]" used to prepare themselves for one hour of contemplation before praying, that their "heart be directed to their Father in heaven."[11] Sustained concentration on the presence of God, towards which prayers were directed, was thus an ideal—though not easily realizable. Realizing this, "One who prays must [ideally] direct his mind in all of them [the benedictions of the *Amidah*]; but if he is unable to direct his mind in all of them he should direct his mind [at the least] in one of them."[12] In these ways there is expressed a manifest attempt to purify a notion that verbal prayer has an effect upon God *just by being spoken.*

In later generations, this theme of purity in prayer was frequently articulated by pietists and moralists.[13] One of these, the great Bahya ibn Paqudah, considers our subject at length, and a portion of his remarks are well worth considering for the light shed on the preferred Jewish attitude towards prayer—which, though it be a fixed duty, and grounded in the assurance of divine attentiveness, is vitally concerned with the purity of prayer and its purifying character. In his very popular tract, *Duties of the Heart,* Bahya states:

> When a man is employed in those duties in which both the heart and the limbs are involved such as prayer and praising God, blessed be He, he should empty himself of all matters appertaining to this world or the next and should empty his heart of every distracting thought . . . He should . . . consider to Whom it is that his prayers are directed and what he intends to ask and what he intends to speak in the presence of his Creator; pondering on the words and their meaning. Know that so far as the language of prayer is concerned the words themselves are like the husk while reflection on the meaning of the words is like the kernel. The prayer itself is like the body while reflection on the meaning is like the spirit, so that, if a man merely utters the words of the prayers with his heart concerned with matters other than prayer, then his prayer is like a body without spirit and a husk without a kernel, because while the body is present when he prays his heart is absent. Of people such as he Scripture says, "For as much as this people draw near, and with their mouth and their lips do honour Me, but have removed their heart far from Me." (Isaiah 29:13)[14]

Many other teachers of Judaism have emphasized this theme. But, together with it, another current—also rooted in the 'expectant certainty' that prayer 'works'—places more stress on the inherent and independent power of the words of prayer, rightly and purely spoken. At first this tendency is largely restricted to virtuosi of the spirit; gradually it became part and parcel of wider Jewish attitudes. Thus, for example, a quite extensive prayer literature has been studied in recent years, and is known as the *Heikhalot* literature, with descriptions of mystical ascents to the divine throne, guided and aided by prayers which protect the ascending spirit through the heavenly spheres, past the negative principalities and forces which hold sway (the archons).[15] These texts of the third and fourth centuries, particularly, not only articulate the majestic Otherness of God on His glorious throne, utterly removed from mankind, but also provide the proper prayerful 'incantations,' as it were—and we may recall the many striking similarities between the language of these prayers and the Greek Magical Papyri[16]—which protect the mystic and assure him of success.

In a related vein, we may further point to the mystical prayers which begin to surface among the later twelfth-century mystics, starting with the celebrated Azriel of Gerona, from whose pen we have one of the earliest Jewish mystical commentaries to the prayer book, in which the proper intentions of the mystic are spelled out.[17] In prayer, properly focused and spoken, the mystic can use the very language of the communal *Siddur* (prayer book) to effect and even restore harmonies in the cosmic sphere, ruptured through primordial spiritual cataclysms. Since the divine realm and its structure of potencies and forces underpin all lower orders of being, the mystic is engaged in an eschatological task—not just a purely 'mystical' one—as he ascends to supernal realms within the Godhead and, with the language of prayer, restores its harmony and order.

You will note, of course, that here the properly lived life of prayer transcends the naïve, literal content of the prayers; that this language—verbal prayer—is but the touchstone and first stage of prayers whose efficacy is of awesome possibilities. Naturally, such mystic exercises were originally for the aristocratic few; but, in the course of the centuries, and particularly after the Jewish exile in Spain, and the new mythic currents which infused the Kabbalah through the teaching of Rabbi Isaac Luria of Palestine, the magical-mystical efficacy of prayers, which is to say their power to effect changes in different parts of the supernal realms of the Godhead, became more and more the property of the many, particularly as new prayer books encoded the mystical-magical symbolism onto the very page. As these prayer books were, in turn, adopted by the eighteenth-century pietist movement known as Hasidism, all this took a more powerful popular turn; but, as we shall see shortly, manipulation of the letters and words of the prayer book came to serve new spiritual purposes.

Be these various processes as they may, and I have alluded to them here so that you have some inkling of the variety of modes in which prayer could be 'relevant' or vital, and the power of verbal prayer as it was understood and used, it is important that we not lose sight of two additional dimensions of prayer in Jewish life: the dimension of *time* and the dimension of *transcendence*. Let me unpack several aspects of these two dimensions which are embedded in our earlier discussion. These comments will also serve to round off our discussion in this part.

As we have seen, the divine initiatives of creation, revelation and redemption are particularly temporal modes: the creation establishes the world and its daily rhythms; revelation establishes a teaching which sanctifies the world and gives it a sacramental character; and redemption establishes the hope for a perfectible world, occurring in time. In prayer, as one dimension of the Jewish way of holiness, the Jew is brought, daily, to an acute consciousness of his being in time, his temporal being. The manifold commandments of the Jewish life pattern, the numerous blessings daily afternoon and evening, during all meals, at the sight of wonders, joys and pains, all sharpen the attentiveness of the Jew to time and its character. In so far as the Jew sustains his life of prayer—which, as we have seen, is fairly indistinguishable from his larger life of religious duty and study, and is often interwoven with it—he is alive to 'time' and to what unfolds in it. Where prayer is engaged truly, there is no 'dead' acceptance of the gifts of the earth, of the movement of the quotidian, of memory of the past. As stressed early, it is not abstract or neutral life that imposes itself upon the Jew in prayer, but immediate and concrete existence.

The dimension of transcendence takes shape in this sphere, but also moves beyond. In one respect, Jewish prayer is a recurrent heightened consciousness of the transcendent Otherness of God, and of one's dependency; but, further, it is through prayer that the individual also transcends the neutrality of existence, engages it directly through blessing, thanksgiving, request and memory. Through prayer, the everyday is raised up; its banality is transcended; and it becomes a context for holiness. In a word, prayer opens an aperture towards eternity, and allows eternity to break into the everyday and transfigure it. The Jew is confirmed, in prayer, that God is the God of eternity, whose bounty and presence are received in time. Blessing acknowledges this eternal God; and simple petition is humbled from this perspective. For what can one really *ask* of eternity, but that it be present? Is not this the heart of petitionary prayer? Is not the core of petitionary prayer the undiminished longing that God's eternal presence be present to us, now? If this is in any respect true, may we add that petitionary prayer is also a species of eschatological yearning—that one wants God, more and more?

The traditional Jew, in his life of pious observance, and particularly in his life of prayer, blesses more and more of the creation; wants more

and more of divine concreteness and bounty and holiness in the everyday; and ceaselessly remembers moments of divine presence and
redemption. In this way the world is lived under the stamp of divinity,
and is inscribed with a prayerful attitude. To the extent that the Jew can
transcend private needs for the sake of the needs of the community and
the world—a dimension which Jewish prayer cultivates in its strong
emphasis on the community of and at prayer, and the strong verbal
emphasis upon "us" and "we" in the prayer book—his yearning for
divine presence is nothing but a yearning for divine actuality: always
and everywhere.

II

As I indicated in my opening comments, this second part of my
discussion will turn to the phenomenon of prayer in the Hebrew
Bible—for there is no doubt that it had a very strong material and
conceptual influence upon the language and religious ideology of rabbinic prayer. Just to bring some of the most compelling and obvious
features of this testimony to your awareness, one may point to the
embodiment—with minor differences—of whole ensembles of psalms
taken from the biblical Psalter in the morning liturgies for the weekday,
the Sabbath and Holy Days. The particular recitation of psalms on a
daily basis is an ancient tradition attested by the earliest stratum of the
Mishnah. The clustering of psalms may reflect a broad range of
features—as they do on weekdays; special elements pertaining to the
special occasion may be found—as in some of the psalms recited on the
Sabbath morning, for example. In addition, special ensembles may be
recited on particular occasions—as the group of psalms recited at the
onset of the Sabbath, at Friday evening, which are marked by the
themes of divine creativity, lordship and universal justice. All these
psalms, as much as any other section of the liturgy, reinforce basic
features of biblical religion and, thereby, serve as the conduit for the
'biblical' ground of rabbinic popular (and official) theology.

Little would be gained here from yet another review of the content
and main types of biblical prayer,[18] or a detailed review of the literary
impact of biblical prayers and psalms on the rabbinic imagination over
the ages—not only in its classical phase, when the basic prayers of the
traditional liturgy were largely put in order and formulated, but also in
later periods, from the Byzantine period on, when a special type of
liturgical poetry—known as *Piyyut*—was composed. Such religious
prayer-poems are intricate and complexly designed—sometimes making use of Arab models, sometimes others, but always reusing and
inventing biblical language and forms. All this belongs to the heart of
Judaism and its continuous prayer life; but it need not be expanded
upon in this context. What, however, I do think appropriate to set forth
here is a phenomenological sketch of aspects of the deep structure of

biblical prayers—such as marks the inner-religious world of the 'biblical person,' and thus underpins the course of Jewish religiosity throughout the ages. It will naturally be impossible to be comprehensive here; but the features and tensions which I shall note, and briefly annotate, do constitute, to my mind, basic elements of biblical prayer, and also set a theological agenda for Judaism and for the modern religious person who sees his theology as biblical—in fact or in origin.

  1. The first phenomenological structure of biblical prayer I shall deal with is that of space; specifically, *the space of Man and the space of God.* For, a focus on the orientation, gesture and direction of prayer has much to reveal with respect to its living dynamics. What is to be noted first of all is that space is humanly constituted *for* prayer and worship: space is not inherently sacred, filled with divinity, or the like. Just as the land is designated as sacred and chosen by God, so are places selected—sometimes by human initiative, sometimes by divine command—as places for worship and prayer. Thus, for example, in the simple yet powerful example which occurs at the beginning of Abram's way of holiness, at Gen 12:8, it is recorded that when the patriarch first came to Beth-El, "he built there an altar to YHWH and called [in prayer] in YHWH's name." This was *his* initiating gesture; quite in contrast to the experience of Jacob, in Gen 28, who fled his father's home and spent a night in the ancient Canaanite sanctuary of Beth-El, only to realize that Elohim was in this place, and he knew it not. Here, the divine initiates the encounter in the world of space, just as He can manifest Himself in the phenomenon of nature, as with Moses at the Thornbush, or in the holiness of the shrine. Surely, this is the context of the theophanies granted Isaiah (ch. 6) and Ezekiel (ch. 1). In less majestic terms, it is the expectation of God's initiating presence in a spatial shrine which has a powerful pull upon all pilgrims who came to Jerusalem—whether to deposit first-fruits and recite a prayerful creed, as in Deut 26, or in the faithful expectation of nearness to God and His blessings, which comes to expression over and over again in the pilgrimage psalms of "Ascent."[19] In these prayers, the pilgrims recite their hopes and expectations; their longings and trust, their memories and anxieties. As one moves towards the center, towards Jerusalem, the dwelling of the Lord, there is a movement closer towards divinity; and it is this which is celebrated in prayer. God's initiating presence—a presence valorized by tradition—in a shrine, in space, gives the prayerful soul direction. One's own space is far or near to the shrine; or one's particular spirit is far or near to the center point, the sacred center, in which God is especially present. Hence, even if one is far from the shrine, in a physical sense or a spiritual one (through sin or transgression), one can initiate a movement and orientation towards the space of God through prayer. Such, at any rate, is the special merit of the Temple of Solomon in Jerusalem; for, to that shrine the worshipper, whether native Israelite or foreigner,

was bidden to pray (1 Kings 8:30, 35, 38, 42; cf. "towards that city which You have chosen and that Temple which You have built for Your name," v. 45).

The orientation and focus of supplications made to God 'in His shrine' are expressed through bodily gestures as well. For, the position of the body in prayer gives a particular locus and gravity to the worshipper who seeks to initiate an address to God. For example, the verb *hishtahaveh* indicates that one might worship prostrate in the shrine before God (cf. Deut 26:10; Isa 27:13), especially in conjunction with sacrificial offerings (1 Sam 1:3). Similarly, one might kneel (*kara^c*) and spread out one's hands to heaven:

> And it was when Solomon had completed praying to YHWH—all this prayer and supplication—he got up from kneeling before the altar with his palms spread out towards heaven (1 Kings 8:54).

Such total physical gestures of supplication and petition, in which the human at prayer reaches out to the heavens, are particularly noteworthy in revealing the spatial axis of prayer. They stress the earth-bound, human facticity of prayer, its direction towards an Other, Who is not of this world—though present in it. The Other-worldly domain of God— also as spatial presence—comes to expression in the biblical notion that God has a Cosmic Shrine, directly above his earthly one, and made in its image (cf. Exod 25:9, 40; 26:30; 27:8). The prayers of mankind are addressed to God in this highest space, as it were; just as it is from this highest space that God can descend and become concretely present in the earthly shrine. The visions of Isaiah (ch. 6) and Ezekiel (ch. 1; 10) attest to such a Temple; and the idea is also reflected in the Psalms (e.g., 29). Similarly, Solomon beseeches God to hear the prayers of Israel and mankind from His cosmic, heavenly shrine (1 Kings 8:30, 39, 43, 49). The same notion comes to expression in the deuteronomic prayer credo of Deut 26:15, when the Israelite brings his first-fruits and requests God to attend from His heavenly abode; and in the days of King Hezekiah, after the Passover ceremonies (2 Chron 30:21-26),

> . . . the priests and Levites arose and blessed the people; and YHWH heard[20] their voice; and their prayer came to His holy, heavenly shrine.

And, finally, it is important to note that there are points where the space of man and God reciprocally incline towards one another, and the formal boundaries of man on earth and God in His shrine are effaced. For, the God of Israel is also "near to all who call upon Him; to all who call upon Him in truth" (Ps 145:18). Hannah calls to God in her hour of need; so does Jonah; and so does Jeremiah. For each, the space of man, the space of his need and supplication, *become* the space of God's presence: for God is called upon to save or answer the supplicant from the situation in which he or she finds himself/herself. If, then, the phenomenological type which we are calling the 'space of God,' as something wholly distinct from the space of man, can help us understand something of the biblical reality of prayer, it is perhaps the fact that, in need, man experiences his space—his human context and *Umwelt*—as bereft of God. The prayer of need is thus *that God come from His space*—from His distance and separateness from man—*and be present in human space*.

By contrast, the joyful soul, full of the awareness of divinity, divine beneficence, or simply the concrete nearness of the divine presence, celebrates that sense of fulness with thanksgiving and praise. In this modality, God's space, as it were, so completely suffuses the space in which the person finds himself, that human, earthly space is transfigured: for, it is suffused with divine everlastingness. If, in the first case, the needful person is aware of his creatureliness and dependence upon God because of the lack and sorrow in his life, in this second case, the thankful person is aware of his creatureliness and dependence upon God because of the bounty which overwhelms him—a bounty he is humble enough to acknowledge as gift and as grace. For such a one, the space of human life is most thoroughly the space of God, always and everlastingly; for the needful one, a dark terror grows in his soul, for the blankness and lack of his life is, for him, the absence of God. His cry of need and request is thus a will to faith; a longing that the silent unyielding earth be for him the context of a holy space, the space of creation, transfigured by divine gifts.

2. As we have seen, the orienting gesture and ritual are tied to the orienting word. This leads to our second structural dynamic: word; specifically, *the word of Man and the word of God*. Reflection on this structure reveals the two basic poles of prayer: man and God. The voice of prayer is always a human voice, a voice from the earth. The speaker is always Man. In petition, language emerges from silence because of God's felt silence: the petitioner asks God to listen, to hear, to attend, to return, to open His eyes, and to answer. All of these terms appear, for example, in the aforementioned prayer of King Solomon; and they are found in many other prayers of officials and common persons. Thus, Man brings his word *to* God. Prayer, in consequence, reveals itself as one-half of a dialogue—petitionary prayer, that is. For, prayers of thanksgiving and praise expect no complementary divine answer. Hereby, the word of man is the bounty of the sated soul, the response to the overwhelming divine initiative. Prayers of thanksgiving thus do not initiate a communication between earth and heaven; for the one reciting praise, the communication *has* been initiated, and the prayer of thanks is the response.

Matters hang altogether differently with respect to petitionary prayer. Hereby, it is man who initiates, and it is God's response—His attention, power, and reaction—which is summoned. Viewed from man's side, which is the side of prayer, the word of petition awaits the word of God. Man may sense that God is absent; or that he has deliberately turned aside and refused prayers (cf. Ps 10:1)—

> You have covered Yourself with a cloud,
> preventing prayer to pass (Lam 3:44).

But, in these ways what is revealed is human need, human confusion and human expectation. For the petitioner, God is not-yet-present; He has not-yet-answered or revealed His 'word.'

The answering word of God is thus the expectation of the individual at prayer. Private prayers—like those of Jonah or Jeremiah—and public prayers—like the petitions of the Psalter—are surrounded by the awesome nimbus of silence. What overwhelmingly resounds in petitionary prayer is the desperate human voice that fills a void (it is not the joyful voice of thanks which sings in concord with the creation). And yet, for certain virtuosi of the spirit, the answering voice is preserved; what the common person awaits, expects and trusts in, is actually made manifest in Scripture. Thus, Moses intercedes in prayer for the people after the episode of apostasy with the Calf, and God accedes; and again later, God acquiesces to Moses' plea and says *salhti kidebarekha* ["I have forgiven, *according to your word* (of request)" (Num 14:20)]. God also responds to Hannah, with a child; to Amos, who requests mercy for his people (cf. Amos 7:2-3, 5-6); though sometimes, the divine answers to say that requests will not be granted, that intercession is vain (Jer 14:11-12, 15:1). But, these are all cases of a special sort. By contrast, was there any way that prayers in the cult were acknowledged as received and accepted by God? There are some indications of this—at least for special occasions, and for special persons, like the king. A striking example of this may be found in 2 Chron 20, where King Jehoshaphat is surrounded by enemies and prays to the Lord for deliverance. Immediately after his request, an officiant of the cult, a Levite, received the spirit of God, and, in a state of ecstasy, pronounced the 'divine' answer: telling the King not to fear, that God would fight with and for him, and to trust in God.

It would be hard to generalize from the preceding case, though other hints lead to the suspicion that some intracultic mechanism existed to communicate the divine word in answer to petitions. Be this as it may, there were other occasions whereby the divine word *initiated* a cultic event. For example, in Psalm 81, we have preserved an old hymn reflecting a covenant renewal ceremony. The people are addressed with their responsibility to the covenant; the Decalogue is paraphrased; and the nation is called upon to return to piety. Significantly, the speaking voice is in the first person (e.g., "*I* am the Lord, your God," v. 11), such that the address to the people was presented as a divine challenge (humanly articulated by priests or prophetical

priests). In this case, it is the divine word which initiates the Psalm, just
as it was the divine presence and promise that initiated Israelite covenantal history. And, it is the human voice which is silent, which is
awaited. The same phenomenon, of a divine voice which confronts the
human worshipper, is found in Psalm 50, as well; and there, too, the
human word is not heard. Man is addressed, and his answer is
'awaited.' What makes these two Psalms all the more arresting is that
while in their original setting it was the initiating word of God that is
dominant, the preservation of these Psalms in the psalter, to be recited
by persons, thoroughly transforms them. They become, to a certain
degree, what they never were: human words addressed to God, human
words which *incorporate* divine words addressed to the nation. In such
prayer, the human voice is addressed to its innermost being; Israel
confronts itself with its tradition and God's challenge. The answer
must equally come from the human side.

   3. We have moved from some consideration of the phenomenology
of space in biblical prayer, to remarks about the phenomenology of the
addressing and receiving word. A more interior structure, one which
often motivates and directs the ways these latter two are actualized, is
that of memory; specifically, *the memory of Man and the memory of God.*
Indeed, so frequently in biblical prayer, the human being at prayer
brings his memory or memories before God as the basis for his petition
and hope; he reminds himself, and, at the same time, reminds God of
His past deeds or promises. The memory can be personal; but, it is
usually more national in nature. Moses, after the episode of the Calf,
reminds God of His promises to the patriarchs—because of the fear
that this promise would be annulled or voided (Exod 32:11-13); similarly, the psalmist, in Psalm 89, reminds God *verbatim* of His promise to
David and his descendants in 2 Samuel 7, and requests that that
promise not be forgotten in the present hour of need, when the king-
ship was threatened (possibly in the course of the Syro-Ephraimite
wars of the late eighth century, B.C.E.); and, again, the psalmist
recites the many acts of Israelite apostasy and corresponding acts of
divine beneficence in the course of Psalm 106—all as a prelude to a
request that these remembered moments serve as a precedent for the
present hour of need, when Israel was in exile, punished for its apostasy, but hopeful of divine grace and deliverance.

   Other national and even cosmic memories are invoked in biblical
prayer; as, for example, those which recall God's salvific and cosmic
power at the creation. Thus, in Isa 51:9-11, the prophet intones an
incantationlike prayer which appeals to God to manifest Himself salvi-
fically in the present just as He did in the past. In so doing, the prophet
invokes older mythic and historical memories:

    Arise! Arise! Put on strength, arm of YHWH;
    Arise, as in days of old, ancient generations.

> Are You not the one that hewed Rahab, and pierced Tanin?
> Are You not the one that shriveled Sea, and the waters
>   of mighty Deep?
> Who made a way through the Sea for the redeemed to pass?
>
> O may the saved of YHWH return;
> May they come to Zion with shouting, garlanded in joy;
> O may happiness and joy drive them on;
> May they rout anguish and woe!

In this prayer, the content of anamnesis—*of* man and *for* God!—is not the acts of the gods *in illo tempore,* which serve as the basis for some ritual mimesis. Rather, the contents of the remembering are unique acts of the Creator-Redeemer God of Israel, at the beginning of time and in historical time. These acts are remembered as the 'rituals' of history. The request of the present invokes God to a renewed encounter with human life; it is enlivened by the confidence that God has been proved powerful and effective in the past. He can, therefore, be trusted to save in the present. One may say that, in the context of prologues which invoke cosmic, and particularly historical acts of saving power (against manifestation of evil and disorder in the past), the petitions of such prayers take the form of minieschatologies. The salvation hoped for is one with restorative dimensions; it is a species of the past and antici- pates the final restoration to come.

Corresponding to this national dimension of memory is the more individual one. The individual petitioner gains courage and confi- dence in his anguish by recalling prior acts of divine beneficence:

> When I call, answer me, My God . . .
> In troubled times You have relieved me;
> Have [now] mercy on me and hear my prayer (Psalm 4:2).
>
> I will thank YHWH with all my heart;
> I will recount all Your wonders . . .
> Be gracious to me, YHWH, behold my torment . . .
> That I might recount all your praises . . .
> And exult in Your salvation (Psalm 9:2; 14-15).

Thus, the psalmist moves from a remembering in the midst of suffer- ing, as the basis of hope in salvation, to a promise to remember, in the hopes that God would be influenced thereby. Man remembers that God was active; and promises to remember God if His salvific be- neficence be granted him in his need. Indeed, this last theme—the promise of praise and remembrance—recurs repeatedly in the Psalter. Man trusts that God does not want to be forgotten, and promises that he will not forget. But, this is not always the case. A sub-modality of the structure of remembrance is that of forgetting; *the forgetting of Man and the forgetting of God*. Man is presented as having forgotten God and His acts of power (for example, Psalms 44:21; 78:11; 106:13, 21); and God is accused, in the pain of the moment, with having forgotten Man (for example, Psalms 10:11 f; 42:10; 44:25; 74:19, 23). Remarkably, prayer is the occasion when such thoughts are expressed. Mankind does not want to be forgotten; but wants his cause and existence remembered:

> Look, YHWH, be not silent;
> My Lord, be not distant from me (Psalm 35:22).

And in token of being remembered, the psalmist concludes:

> . . . My mouth shall speak of Your vindication;
> [It shall recount] Your praise all the day (v. 28).

4. One more phenomenological structure of biblical prayer may be noted in this framework: power; specifically, *the power of Man and the power of God*. Since this is a far-reaching dynamic, I shall briefly refer to but one feature of it: the issue of justice. The petitioner comes before God with a sense of justice, and wants that sense vindicated: for this would be a concrete, worldly expression of divine power. Thus, the person refers to YHWH as a god of justice (cf. Psalms 7:12; 9:5); as one who loves justice (33:5; 89:15; 97:2); and as one who takes account of injustice. For this reason, man approaches God as a petitioner demanding justice (Psalms 7:7, 9; 9:8, 17; 26:1; 35:24; 37:28, 30); he even recites eschatological prayers about justice—as in Psalm 82.

This appeal for human justice and justification is further linked to the appeal for salvation—for *yeshuᶜah*.

> Arise, YHWH! Save me, my God (Psalm 3:8).

> Save me, for Your honor's sake (Psalm 6:5).

> Shine Your presence, that we be saved (Psalm 80:4, 8).

The prophet Jeremiah also cries, "heal me that I may be healed; save me that I may be saved" (17:14); and both the psalmist and Jeremiah want salvation from their enemies (cf. Psalm 7:2; Jer 17:18). They expect it; they request it; they even demand it because YHWH is a god of justice—and "does not the God of all the earth perform justice?" In fact, this expectation of divine vindication, and the sense of self-righteousness which often accompanies it, help explain the particular aggressiveness of many of the Psalms of petition, and their often thunderous use of curses (as in Psalms 69 and 109). The worshipper's stance is particularly forceful and vengefully confident because he believes himself to have been obedient and observant—the victim of injustice which *will* be avenged.

Of course, the positive side of this religious modality is *trust,* and this is a frequent and important element in biblical prayers (cf. Psalms 13:6; 22:5; 28:7).

I have trusted Your words (Psalm 119:42).

Hear me . . . for I have trusted in You (Psalm 143:8).

But, here the fuller dynamic must be brought out. This sub-modality of power, which trusts in God because He is the superior cosmic power, has a negative aspect: *shame.* If trust emerges as an expression of confidence that the righteousness of one's case will be vindicated because God is a god of Right, and the Redeemer, shame is the fear or presentiment that this trust has been misplaced, that YHWH may not be or choose to be the god of power who will vindicate him. The shame is expressed as a shame in one's own eyes (cf. Jer 13:19; Ezra 9:6), and in the eyes of others (Jer 9:18; Psalm 31:2, 18). Indeed, the psalmist often uses this point—the shame of shame!—in his petitions to God to manifest His justice, lest the nations think that He can do no other, that He is not a god of Justice and Right.

Accordingly, man's sense and fear of shame reveal a potential rupture in trust and expectation of divine beneficence. It reveals man as fearful; as unconfident, hesitant, and anxious about the reality of divine power. It reveals him as one who prays trustingly to a god of power because he—the human—is powerless! And now he fears that he has misplaced that trust (Job 6:20); or that that trust has been betrayed! Shame, in the context of prayer, reveals an incongruity between past belief (and its expectations) and present reality. The deuteronomic theology, with its rationalizing emphasis on curse and blessing and divine providence, did much to alleviate this fear and the incongruities of God's presence; it did much to promote confidence in a dependable covenant and in divine justice. But, the Psalms are not a generalizing theology. They rather reflect the living soul in time, with all its anxieties, its ruptures of faith, and its disorientations at those moments where justice seems far off and trust is only a memory of past faith. At such moments, the legal structure of many prayers, with their expectation of vindication, is undercut: for God's silence lurks as the possibility of divine abandonment and—worse of all—impotence. These prayers disclose mankind as it really is: fearful and often feeling bereft; and they challenge God to be who He really is—or at least as Tradition remembers Him to have been.

III

Of course, very much more could be said about biblical prayer; but, our purpose is not to be comprehensive as much as it is to disclose some

of the living dynamics of biblical man before God in prayer—
dynamics, as remarked, which are basic to Judaism as well. In addition, very much more could be said about prayer in Judaism itself. For,
indeed, we have referred only to verbal prayer, and not at all to the
great tradition of contemplative prayer as it emerged in the high Middle Ages—among moralists, philosophers and Kabbalists—and as it
came to particularly vigorous and renewed expression in the early
generations of Hasidism, in the middle of the eighteenth century. In
that latter tradition, verbal prayer is but a *means* to something higher
and more spiritual. Verbal prayer is not denied; nor could it be. For, as
we earlier remarked, prayer is the very basis of Jewish communal
worship: a positive religious duty in rabbinic Halakha. But beyond
this, in early Hasidism, prayer is actually a means to spiritual eleva-
tions and absorption in the Godhead. For the Maggid of Mezeritch, an
early Hasidic master, contemplative prayer was the ideal, even to the
derogation of verbal prayer. As the words of conventional verbal
prayer are rooted in divine mysteries, as the letters are concretizations
of supernal potencies, the mystic, in prayer, must seek to "enter the
words," properly combine the letters into permutations congruent
with the divine name and supernal mysteries, and thereby ascend
beyond the world of space and time, beyond the constraints of ego, to
the divine realms of Logos and Sophia—and beyond. The self annihi-
lates its concrete ego-nature and, by attaching itself to the spiritual core
within the material words of prayer, descends into the bosom of infin-
ity, into God Himself, into the God beyond—not the *deus revelatus,* but
the *deus absconditus.*[21]

In such prayer, the old concreteness of biblical and rabbinic prayer—
exoteric prayer—is effaced: there is truly nothing to ask for; and praise
is truly vain. The divine initiative is so full, so comprehensive, that the
only true religious task is to adhere to the fulness of the divine
pleroma—to annihilate one's self into it. Here, prayer withdraws from
the concreteness of life that the praying person be filled with God; here,
prayer obliterates petition and praise as acts of ego. For meditative
prayer, petitions and praise only maintain the distance between man
and God—a distance which the Maggid believed to be illusory. With
spiritual training, that distance may be closed, and all earthly needs
and joys are revealed for what they truly are within the bosom of
eternity: expressions of the small ego.

I shall not pursue this matter further here. As daring and remarkable as is this tradition within Judaism—and there are many other
expressions of it in philosophical writings as well—the fact remains that
the exoteric tradition of prayer was never denied or denigrated entirely.
Even Maimonides, a philosophical contemplative, strongly influenced
by Aristotle, and master of great arguments against the notion that
God—the Unmoved Mover—could be influenced by prayer, and thus
change, wrote compendia of rules about prayer, and prayed. In his

Mishneh Torah we have comprehensive formulations of the official requirements of prayer. If his philosophical path was that of the *via negativa,* denying all positive attributes of God such that the only true prayer is silence, his religious path was a *via activa,* filled with the language of prayerful praise and petition. Indeed, in one remarkable incident, when at sea and in a tempest, the great Maimonides prayed petitions and vowed a yearly fast if he were delivered—a vow he lived to fulfill. Just how this great philosopher reconciled his religious and philosophical positions has been a matter of constant debate.[22] I note the contradiction here solely in order to stress that, as tempting as it would be to focus on the phenomenon of contemplative silence, or mystical self-annihilation, exoteric prayer, verbal prayer, was a basic building block of traditional Judaism, and an unfactorable part of its life of prayer. To obscure its character, biblically derived, would do a great disservice to our task at this Institute: which is to focus on those perspectives on prayer which have joined Jew to Jew over the course of the generations, and which form the popular and inherent Jewish theology of the ages.

The exoteric prayer book is the soul of living Judaism. Many spiritual giants have descended to secret chambers of this soul, to silent and lonely caverns of its innermost life; but, they have done so with the full knowledge that even the exoteric prayers guided them inward to special states of divine nearness. In finding the super-soul, they never denied the soul.

IV

In the course of my discussion, I have referred to many theological dimensions. I shall not try to recapitulate them here, or estimate their value for modern Jews. Let me rather share with you some elements and dimensions of Jewish prayer which are theologically important to me—a modern Jew: one who is religious, but not in any simple traditional sense; and one who prays, who tries to pray, and who hopes to really pray again.

In Judaism, as we have seen, prayer stands in an essential relationship to life: it is part of the daily ritual; it makes its mark in every sphere of life, and it orients the Jew to time—prayers are fixed in the morning, afternoon and evening—and to the events which transpire around him. The life of prayer in Judaism thus cultivates, in a certain respect, a prayerful attitude towards life and existence. In what follows I shall extract from all this certain elements which are particularly important to me—these do not substitute for prayer, but, rather, indicate how the ideals of Jewish prayer inform my life in a central degree.

1. My first point is that prayer is a *vehicle of orientation towards the divine,* towards God. Prayer is a response to a received world: perhaps a world brimming with meaning, perhaps one with apparent lack and

disorder: but a world which I receive as a creature, not of my making. Prayer, then, is at once a mode of acknowledging and a mode of naming. In the first case, I am inspired by a motif that appears several times in early rabbinic literature which emphasizes that the person who does not bless or thank God for the realities of life and the world, is nothing other than a thief—one who takes what is not his.[23] To receive the world, to orient myself towards it in thanksgiving and in need, is to cultivate my creatureliness and God's creatorhood. In the second case, that of naming, I think of myself as a descendant of Adam: he who received the world and gave it names, and thus oriented himself towards it. For myself, such an image is meaningful, for thereby I come to regard myself as a being who must regard the world afresh, and name it in relationship to God. When I conceive of prayer as a form of naming and describing my existence, I understand it as a modality which orients me towards God as the Creator. In prayer, I am able to transcend myself as a single one, and to acknowledge my creaturehood within the framework of the everlastingness and immediacy of the world. Moreover, by addressing myself towards the Creator as a You, I acknowledge that the creation is not something neutral to me, nor is God's creative presence something neutral to me: the neutrality of life is transcended as I say 'You' to God in prayer.

2. My addressing word in prayer, my addressing life of prayer, enables me to engage the world of divine creation as something more than the concrete occasions of life; it enables me to engage it as the totality of eternity which I touch and feel, but which ever resists my final naming of it. As I sense this, I try to gather the full resources of my being in every utterance; I try to bring my whole self towards God and His eternity—not my partial and fragmentary self. In the language of the rabbis, I try to make my mouth and heart of one accord.[24] This brings me to my second point, which is that prayer is *emblematic of life.* By this I mean that my ability to address myself wholly, in a unifying way, towards God in prayer is indicative of, and a challenge to, the degrees of integrity which I manifest in other areas of life. The Hasidic masters, from the Baal Shem Tov on, were fond of reinterpreting a scriptural statement made in the Book of Genesis, with respect to Noah. It says there that he went into the ark (*tebah*); and this phrase was punningly reinterpreted in light of the rabbinic use of the word *tebah* to mean "word." Noah's paradigmatic piety was such, we might say, that he fully entered the word of prayer, as we must also do or try to do. To fully enter the words of prayer is to be fully present to the words and occasions at hand; and it is a correlative of the ideal to enter fully the words and occasions of life in all their diversity.

In some measure, one might say that in this regard prayer is preparatory for life, insofar as it seeks to cultivate a unification of mouth and heart, of inner and outer being at all times. From this perspective, interiority in prayer, the descent inward, is not a descent into God as

the innermost self, away from the world, but, rather, a descent into the
recesses of silence, there to cultivate an inner strength which manifests
itself in speech which is direct and pure, whose inner harmony greets
the world in a unifying attitude. Where my prayer life is alienated from
true harmony, where my mouth and thoughts are separate, I cannot
hope that my life before God, and in the world, will have much harmony. And, where I cannot put myself wholly into an 'I' that speaks to
a divine 'You,' as the unity of all existence, there may be little hope that
much of my life and its words will be more than chatter and fragments.

3. A third point I would like to make has its point of departure in the
notion called in early Hasidism: "the elevation of strange thoughts."
The Hasidic masters, as all spiritual teachers, were acutely aware of the
difficulty in maintaining *kavvanah,* of focused attentiveness to God, in
prayer. The mind wanders; it is filled by distracting fears and anticipa-
tions; and becomes disoriented. The urge to communicate with God,
which is fostered and encouraged by prayer, breaks down into a return
to the self, into small goals and small desires. The self turns upon the
self, not towards God. The contents of these distracting thoughts and
fantasies vary, of course. In early Hasidism, the torment of unfocused
prayer was great, for great was the desire to be with God in prayer.
Accordingly, early masters taught that, when one was obsessed by
thoughts not germane to the prayer content, one should not simply try
to repress them, but rather stay with them, understand their content—
say physical needs, erotic fantasies, desires for power, and so on—and
try to link them to their supernal source in the divine world—say to the
potencies of the divine which is the source of sustenance, or the forces
which bind dimensions of the world to each other, or the source of all
potencies, and so on.

The concern is to elevate the distracting thoughts to their divine
ground, as it were; to transcend the self; to see oneself as a participant
in energies, desires and forces which emanate from the divine worlds.
Thereby one may bring the disquieting 'thoughts' to rest, and return
the self to a divine perspective.[25] In the process of elevating strange
thoughts, one struggles to return to the divine Self—away from the
petty self; away from the small ego and its concerns. Of course, staying
with those distracting feelings, whatever they are, is dangerous, as
opponents of this 'spiritual' practice were acutely aware—for one
might succumb to their baser forms. For this and other reasons, the
practice of 'elevation' of strange and distracting thoughts was modi-
fied, if not suspended, in later Hasidism.

I am not here advocating a return to such notions. But, I do want to
raise a point or two that seem to me important. Particularly, I wish to
state that, since prayer is a desire for pure speech and relationship,
distracting and alien thoughts are an index and reflex of the confusions
of mind of the person at prayer. For me, at any rate, whenever distractions break down my concentration in prayer, they are usually a good

indication of my fragmented soul. The thoughts that may preoccupy me, or the concerns, are usually related to my 'small ego,' my petty achievements and station in the world, the limited perspectives I can have about my life among people and institutions, and the like. By having a check on these ideas, which erupt into the silence and singleness of prayer, I become acutely aware of my spiritual level and state.

I would hardly go so far as to say that there is some divine communication here; but, I would be willing to say that as I address my self to God, the You that embraces and vitalizes all earthly yous, there can be some action of my self upon my self through the language of prayer; there can be some interior communication *to me* as I become aware *in prayer* of the points where my attention folds back upon itself and becomes concerned with my self, my ego needs, and so on. When these disruptions and energies are quieted—by regarding them from the standpoint of God, from the perspective of eternity and the divine pleroma from which all flows and is enlived—my 'self' is transcended for the sake of God; for the sake of a larger attitude towards the world and creation; for the sake of eternity. My distractions in prayer are thus a teaching to me in the depths of myself, as I struggle to see everything as part of the divine reality. They are a clue to my idolatries and sins against the spirit. Inevitably, similar distractions and 'ego-games' intervene and disrupt my communication with other humans in the world. But, of these I am not always aware. It is prayer that helps make me aware of them.

4. A final matter—partially related to the preceding. While true prayer is always an attempt to stand before God purely, the modes differ. I should like, in closing, to address one of these modes, and do so via a personal exegesis of Psalm 50. As you will recall from my remarks in Part II, this psalm was not originally a prayer, in any meaningful sense, but rather a divine proclamation—through the appointed teachers and disciples—to Israel to heed the covenant. Only secondarily, as this piece became part of the psalter and its corpus of prayers, did Psalm 50 become a prayer of sorts. Let us see what this means; and also what it may mean to a contemporary person of faith.

A brief review of Psalm 50 reveals the following structure: verses 1-6 announce that YHWH is God, the Creator, and appears from Zion. They further state that YHWH appears in order to judge His people, and then invokes all the covenanters of Israel to assemble before their judge. Even here, the complex setting of this psalm is evident: for, while one cultic voice announces YHWH as a judge, in v. 5 another voice speaks in the first person. This variation suggests that different 'official' cultic spokesmen present the contents of the psalm to the public—and one of these actually speaks for the Lord Himself. The second part of the psalm continues from this point, in vv. 7-23. Here, the divine voice, through the designated spokesman, calls the people to judgment, brings forth the divine testimony, and states that ''I am

Your God." With these latter words, which allude to the Decalogue, and the preceding references to divine testimony, it is clear that the people are arraigned in some cultic or festival ceremony. A precise parallel occurs in Ps 81, where a divine testimony is first given, in similar language (cf. Ps 81:9), and then the opening lines of the Decalogue follow (cf. especially, "I, YHWH, am Your God," v. 11).

The divine rebuke in Psalm 50 continues with the statement that the Lord will not reprove the people for their *zebah*—sacrifices—for their sacrificial performances: for He is the Lord of all creation, and what need has He for the creatures of the earth returned to Him in sacrifice? What YHWH wants, however, is acknowledgment (and the sacrifices which may accompany it), the fulfillment of vows, and supplication (see vv. 14-15). At this point, the interlocutor continues ("and against the evil one God said," v. 16), and states YHWH's criticism of the transgressors: who are hypocrites, who purport to accept the divine law but avoid it at every turn. God's word is disregarded when one joins in complicity with thieves and adulterers; when one oppresses others through speech or deception, and the like (see vv. 17-19). For these things the nation will be held accountable (see v. 21, and compare v. 8). Only those who sacrifice thanksgiving offerings, and set their path with the Lord in truth, can hope to receive divine beneficence. All others will be destroyed—nothing will avail them (cf. vv. 21-23).

As I said, the life-setting for this proclamation was possibly some cultic context of opprobrium; or possibly a covenant-renewal ceremony. That it is not simply a prophetic rebuke for covenantal transgressions is clear from the fact that it is dignified in an official liturgical framework. Undoubtedly, spokesmen for the cult and the shrine were allied with the aims and language of prophecy; or, just the opposite, it is possible that certain prophetic guilds were trained in the shrine and served its purposes. Whatever the original historical setting—and while this is obscure in detail, the wider ambiance seems clear enough—it is certain that Psalm 50 was not originally a prayer. As stated, it was at first a teaching and rebuke within the cult; it becomes a 'prayer' only through its contextual association with other prayers— *and by its prayerful recitation over the generations.*

So now, finally, we come to the central question. What does (or might) it mean to pray this psalm? To me, this would mean a prayer of self-judgment; a prayer in which one held oneself accountable for the purity of one's religious life. Insofar as there is a divine voice which occurs in the prayer, one's self is, *in prayer,* confronted by the God of tradition, and by the living God, and held accountable. One must ask oneself prayerfully: Do I simply perform acts of divine obedience routinely? Am I a hypocrite? Am I a religious conniver, a master of deceit? As noted earlier, there is no human response in the original psalm; correspondingly, there is no final answer in my praying of it. Each recitation of Psalm 50 undermines and criticizes the preceding ones. I must ask: am I reciting this prayer wholeheartedly? Indeed, as prayer, Psalm 50 forces me to ask whether my own self-judgment is honest, or whether it is framed in deceit.

The prayer is thus unending: it opens into life. Its true shape is the thorough internalization of its challenge, so that my entire life may become a living of this prayer: a constant striving for honesty before God; a constant struggle against deception and irresponsibility; a constant challenge to give to God what truly belongs to him. But, what does this God want? Honesty in relationship? Yes; and more. He wants sacrifices of thanksgiving; and so, simultaneously, an acknowledgment of His creatorhood and a deep awareness of one's creaturehood. Such a divine demand, demanded in and through the language of Psalm 50, excludes prayers and sacrifices of petition. For, I am a creature, and what in the creation can I sacrifice and give to Him? Myself? My will— in thanksgiving, or through the actions of the covenant? For the psalmist, the answer is clear—certainly more certain than it is for me. For though, as a Jew, I have the teachings of YHWH as received and interpreted by tradition, I still ask: How should these be brought before the Lord? And, what does religious humility truly require? In some sense, Psalm 50 is a mantra along the way. It does not answer these or other questions, but it does help undermine idolatries for the sake of true piety. Like Jewish prayer generally, Psalm 50 is a challenge to convert prayer into prayerful living.

NOTES

[1] The important Hebrew work by J. Heinemann, *Prayer in the Talmud* (Studia Judaica, ix; Berlin & New York: W. de Gruyter, 1977), has now been translated into English, and the interested reader will find there a wealth of information on the formation and formulation of early Jewish prayer; and a fine general bibliography in European languages.

[2] *Weekday Prayer Book,* ed. J. Harlow (New York: The Rabbinical Assembly of America, 1962), pp. 10-13.

[3] *Weekend Prayer Book,* ed. J. Harlow (New York: The Rabbinical Assembly of America, 1962), pp. 42-45.

[4] *Wisdom of Solomon* 11:23-12:1. This translation, based on R.H. Charles's *Apocrypha and Pseudepigrapha* and the Authorized Version, is found in *Language of Faith,* ed. N. Glatzer (New York: Schocken Books, 1975), p. 34.

[5] Cf. *Tanhuma, Vezot Haberakah,* VII, and elsewhere.

[6] Cp. the translation in Glatzer, *op. cit.,* p. 52.

[7] By Joseph Brenner; see S. Spiegel, *Hebrew Reborn* (New York: Meridian Books and the Jewish Publication Society of America, 1962), p. 354; cf. Glatzer, *ibid.,* p. 59.

[8] *Weekday Prayer Book,* pp. 45-46.

[9] Chapter XVIII; translation from Glatzer, *Language of Faith,* p. 50.

[10] *Weekday Prayer Book,* pp. 49-52.

[11] *Mishnah Berakhot* V:1; cf. Babylonian Talmud, tractate *Berakhot* 31a.

[12] See Babylonian Talmud, tractate *Berakhot* 34b.

[13] See, for example, H.G. Enelow, "Kawwanah: the Struggle for Inwardness in Judaism," in *Studies in Jewish Literature in honor of Kaufmann Kohler* (Berlin: G. Reimer, 1913), pp. 82-107.

[14] *Hasidic Prayer,* trans. L. Jacobs (New York: Schocken Books, 1973), pp. 71-72.

[15] See G. Scholem, *Jewish Gnosticism, Merkabah Mysticism, and Talmud Tradition* (New York: Jewish Theological Seminary, 1960), *passim,* with representative selections in the appendices.

[16] *Ibid., passim.*

[17] See G. Sed-Rajna, *Commentaire sur la liturgie quotidienne, [par] Azriel de Gerone* (Etudes sur le judaïsme médiéval, V; Leiden: E.J. Brill, 1974); also see the earlier, seminal essay of G. Scholom, "Der Begriff der Kawwana in der alten Kabbala," *Monatschrift für Geschichte und Wissenschaft des Judentums* 78 (1934), pp. 492-518.

[18] The reader interested in prayer in the Psalter may turn to such works as H. Gunkel's classic, *Einleitung in die Psalmen,* ed. J. Begrich (Göttingen: Vandenhoeck & Ruprecht, 1933); *The Psalms* (Facet Books 19; Philadelphia: Fortress Press, 1967); also N. Füghster, *Das Psalmengebet* (München: Kösel, 1965); and C. Westermann, *The Praise of God in the Psalms* (Richmond, Va.: J. Knox, 1965). For prayer outside the Psalter, of basic value are A. Wendel, *Das Frei Laiengebet im vorexilischen Israel* (Leipzig: Pfeiffer, 1932), and Y. Kaufmann, *Toledot Ha-emunah Ha-yisra'elit* II/2 (Tel Aviv: Dvir, 1945), pp. 499-506 (abridged in *The Religion of Israel* [Chicago: Univ. of Chicago Press, 1960], pp. 309-11). Of recent interest is M. Greenberg's essay, "On the Refinement of the Conception of Prayer in Hebrew Scriptures," *Association for Jewish Studies Review* 1 (1976), pp. 57-92.

[19] Cf. Psalm 122, and my discussion of it in my *Text and Texture, Close Readings of Selected Biblical Texts* (New York: Schocken Books, 1979), Ch. 8, "Psalm 122/ Space in Suspension: The Pilgrimage," pp. 103-7.

[20] Reading with the Syriac version, and assuming an abbreviation in the Massoretic Text.

[21] See, for example, J. Weiss, "The Kavvanoth of Prayer in Early Hasidism," *Journal of Jewish Studies* 9 (1958), pp. 163-92; R. Schatz, "Contemplative Prayer in Hasidism," in *Studies in Mysticism and Religion Presented to G. Scholem* (Jerusalem: Magnes Press, 1967), pp. 209-26; L. Jacobs, *Hasidic Prayer,* pp. 70-92.

[22] See the excellent survey of this problematic in Maimonides's oeuvre, with many source citations, by M. Fox, "Prayer in Maimonides' Thought," in *Prayer in Judaism: Continuity and Change,* ed. G. Cohen (Jerusalem: Ahvah Ltd., 1978), pp. 142-67 (in Hebrew).

[23] See above, n. 5.

[24] See Babylonian Talmud, tractate *Berakhot* 13a.

[25] For a clear treatment of this subject, see L. Jacobs, *Hasidic Prayer,* pp. 104-20.

Jesus' Response to God as Abba: Prayer and Service

John Shea

The topic to be tackled is Jesus' naming of his experience of God as Abba and how that experience eventuates in a life of prayer and service. We will explore this under three headings. First, we will consider the reason Christians return to the story of Jesus. What do we hope to gain by remembering the life of the founder? In particular, what purpose is there in retrieving and inhabiting one of his major metaphors for the experience of God—Abba? Secondly, since Abba is an image which hopes to express and communicate a religious experience, some of the ground rules for the interpretation of symbols should be spelled out. We will look at some of the logical moves that go on between religious experience and its expression in image and story. Thirdly, we will penetrate the image of Abba in the hope of experiencing the divine reality which lurks there. Then, we will re-articulate that experience in new language and attempt to detail the style of service and prayer which flows from it.

THE MEMORY OF JESUS: HEARTBREAK AND HOPE

The origins of Christianity are a matter of much dispute. Thesis and counter-thesis abound. But, the poet's penetration of the productly perverse accounts of scripture intuits a story of heartbreak and hope. Of course, where there is heartbreak, there need be love at first. And of course, where there is hope, there need be love at last.

First, there is the heartbreak of Jesus and his hope. Chapters 13-17 of the gospel of John are the last will and testament of a dying man. It is the story of Jesus, the man who wanted to stay but had to go. Jesus must go to drink wine in the Kingdom of his Father; but, he wants to

stay and drink wine in the company of his friends. To overhear this
final conversation, even with its heavy theological accents, is to sense
its emotional power:

> My little children,
> I shall not be with you much longer.
> You will look for me,
> And where I am going,
> You cannot come.

His friends will search for Jesus, the one they love, but they will not
find him. He must journey to a far place, and they cannot accompany
him. Yet, in the vision of the Johannine Christ even this loss turns to
gain:

> I will not leave you orphans . . .
> You are sad at heart.
> Still, I must tell you the truth:
> It is for your own good that I am going,
> Because, unless I go,
> The advocate will not come to you; but if I do go,
> I will send him to you.

This advocate is the spirit of truth, a witness to Jesus and sent from the
Father. Jesus must go, but the spirit will remain. So, the heartbreak of
departure gives way not only to the hope of reunion:

> In a short time you will no longer see me
> And then a short time later you will see me again.

but, to a new mode of presence:

> The spirit will glorify me
> Since all he tells you
> Will be taken from what is mine.
> Everything the Father has is mine;
> That is why I said:
> All he tells you
> Will be taken from what is mine.

So, the fundamental Christian paradox emerges. The one who is not
here is here; the one who had to go manages to stay; the one who drinks
wine at the right hand of the Father also drinks the wine of earth with
his latest band of followers.

It took centuries for the Christian church to develop a full blown
doctrine of the Trinity. The path of this development was long and
tortuous, bringing together the abstract intellects and violent emotions
of many Christians. And, once the trinitarian doctrine was fully

formed, speculation on its meaning and implications has been extensive. But, in its embryonic form in the gospel of John it seems to
function as the most adequate understanding of the fact that the experience of God which Jesus made possible continues within the community even after Jesus had returned to the Father. And, since Jesus was
the originator of this experience and was intimately and unbreakably
linked with its continuance, wherever this experience happened, Jesus
must be there in some way. But, Jesus is manifestly not there in the way
he once was—flesh and bones. Therefore, he must be there in a new
way. He is present through the Spirit whom the Father sent in his
name. One function of the doctrine of the Trinity is that it expresses the
assurance that even though Jesus is not present in the way he once was,
the experience of God he made possible is still available.

Secondly, there is the heartbreak of the disciples and their hope.
Although all the evangelists intimate that the resurrection appearances
came to an end, it is Luke who dramatizes this fact through the ascension narratives. In the story that concludes the gospel of Luke, the risen
Christ commissions his disciples to be witnesses of his life, death and
resurrection and urges them to stay in the city until "they are clothed
with power from on high." Then, he is carried up into heaven, and
"the disciples returned to Jerusalem with great joy; and they were
continually in the Temple praising God."

Yet, in the ascension story that begins the Acts of the Apostles a
slightly different rendition is given. The sight of the disappearing
Christ does not spur the disciples to the temple to prayer and praise.
Rather, as Jesus is lifted up and a cloud takes him out of sight, they
stand there gazing into the heavens. Luke tells us that two men clothed
in white, symbols of the resurrection, chide them: "Men of Galilee,
why do you stand looking into heaven? This Jesus who was taken up
from you into heaven will come in the same way as you saw him go into
heaven." This second rendition suggests a poignancy to the departure
of Christ, a sense of loss on the part of the disciples, a heartbreak that
must find hope.

The question of the two men in white robes, "Why do you stand
staring at the sky?," seems a shade insensitive. It is probably meant as
an encouragement to greater faith. "Do not be sad. The one who has
left will soon return. Do not doubt. Do not brood over your loss. Do not
be paralyzed. The departed one will soon be the returning one." Even
so, as the goodbye scenes at every airport and railway station attest, the
conviction of reunion is scant consolation for the loss of presence.

If we look at this farewell narrative from the perspective of the
affective dimension of human nature, their standing and staring are
not difficult to understand. It is merely what people who have lost
something important do. I was once told the story of a woman who
rewrote the story of Lot's wife in the Old Testament. Her rendition
went this way:

Mr. Lot came home and said to Mrs. Lot, "I have seen the Lord."
        "Sure," said Mrs. Lot.
        "No, I have really," said Mr. Lot. "And he told me that we
must leave these wicked cities."
        "Wicked cities?," said Mrs. Lot. "But if the Lord says so."
        And so, Lot's wife went out to her friends and neighbors,
embraced them for the last time and told them of her plans to leave.
Then, she hunted down her children who were playing with their friends
and dragged them home to prepare them for the journey. Next, she went
to her animals, her pets, and fed them for the last time. Then, she took
down from the walls of her house all the things that had turned it into a
home. She packed everything she had in saddle bags; and she and Lot
and the children journeyed out into the desert to which God calls all
people to at one time or another.

The woman finished the story with this line, "Of course she looked
back." That story parallels the affective tone of the ascension narrative
in Acts. "Why do you stand and stare at the sky?" They stand and
stare at the sky because their home has left.

When Jesus was with them, in both his earthly life and in his risen
appearances, they found a possibility of living they had never experienced before. They stand and stare at the sky because they wonder
whether the possibility of life that was theirs when Jesus was with them
will leave with the one who gave it to them. The underlying dilemma of
the entire New Testament is that Jesus leaves twice. The first time he
leaves into the realm of death. At this leaving his disciples are dis-
banded, dispirited, and frightened. He returns from the realm of
death, and their cowardice turns to courage, their fear finds hope, and
their panic become peace. Then, he leaves a second time. Their question is inevitable. Will the power and love and freedom that Jesus made
possible go with him into the sky? What will happen in the wake of the
second leaving?

It is in this situation of heartbreak that the first and perennial
Christian strategy is devised. The logic of the process could be
paraphased as follows: "Perhaps if we do the things that Jesus did when
he was with us, the experience of God that he made possible will still be
available to us. What did he do when he was with us? He told us stories.
Let us remember the stories that Jesus told us and tell those stories
again. And, in the telling of the stories, perhaps we may find that the
way we experienced ourselves, each other, and our life will return. We
must remember the stories. For, in the memory of the stories is the
presence of the person. But, not only the stories Jesus told. We must
formulate accounts of his entire life, of all the things he underwent and
overcame. If we remember the stories he told and tell the stories about
what he did, the power of God which was present then will continue to
be present now in new and startling ways. What else did Jesus do when

he was with us? He ate and drank with us and, in the eating and drinking, we found a solidarity and a power we had never experienced before. Perhaps now if we eat and drink with one another in his name, his presence will come among us again, and the power of God identified with his presence will once again flood our lives." In the middle of heartbreak this is the Christian wager of hope. Gather the folks, break the bread, drink the wine, tell the stories. And so, there is developed the core myth and ritual of Christianity through which the experience of God which Jesus of Nazareth made possible is continued in space and time.[1]

Christians live in the strategies of hope that Jesus and the first disciples devised. These strategies and the living religious tradition of Christianity in general attempt to pass on to succeeding generations the experience of God which founded the faith. A religious tradition is a diverse and complex phenomenon.[2] It contains cognitive claims which seek to state the truth about reality. Christian faith affirms: "God created the world," "Humankind needs grace to be saved," "In Christ God was reconciling the world to himself," etc. Along with cognitive claims there are value statements and their embodiments in diverse historical settings. Christian faith values justice and tries to make it operative in the areas of work, war, and wealth. It proclaims love and tries to make it concrete in guidelines about marriage and sex. But, the cognitive claims and preeminent values of Christian faith are grounded in a specific experience of God. To remember the life of the founder goes beyond holding convictions and prizing values. Its ambition is to participate in the religious experience that generated the faith tradition.

This rendition of remembering and re-experiencing stresses the logical priority of soteriology over christology.[3] The salvific impact Jesus had on people and the continued availability of that impact through the narratives of the gospels precede the question of his identity. Who he is is important only because of what he is capable of making happen. The human condition seems to be characterized by the fact that we are interested in the identity only of those people who are bringing us to new and creative possibilities. The story of the tempest at sea (Mk. 4:35-41) captures this procedure. Jesus and his disciples are in the boat. Jesus is asleep. A storm comes up. The disciples are terrified. They wake Jesus and ask him to help. He rebukes them for their lack of faith, calms the winds and sea, and goes back to sleep. In this situation the disciples ask, "Who is this that even the winds and sea obey him?" The suggestion is that if Jesus had been washed overboard, they would never have asked. We pursue the identity of those people in whose presence we sense we are saved.

The purpose, therefore, of our retrieval of one of Jesus' core images for God, Abba, is to uncover the specific religious experience it expresses and hopes to communicate. Our interest in the religious experience of Jesus is not motivated by the lofty ideal of accurate historical reconstruction. Although the results of historical scholarship will be consulted, our persevering interest is that of followers seeking to be initiated into the salvific experience of the master. This is an exploration from within the living Christian tradition which hopes to mine one of its main metaphors. When we dwell within the image of Abba and come into contact with the divine reality it "houses," we will enter into our relationship with God in a specific way. Out of this experience will come a way of prayer and action that are Christian because they are indebted to the Christian formulation of divine-human interaction. This is what we are about. But, first we must investigate the "twists and turns" of the relationship among religious experience, metaphor, and story.

RELIGIOUS EXPERIENCE: IMAGE AND STORY

The literature on religious experience is vast and diversified.[4] There is no easy way to "corral" it. For our purposes we can isolate some characteristics and unfold some of the consequences of religiously significant experiences.

Religious experiences are those special moments when we become aware we are related to a transcendent otherness. In and through the finite realities that we immediately encounter we sense the presence of a sacred power.[5] Our consciousness is expanded;[6] and a baffling rush of insight and feeling overtakes us.[7] We have a felt-perception of the Mystery of life itself.[8] In this moment of experience we sense that we are receivers and not initiators. The experience is given to us and not produced by us.[9] In the words of Paul Tillich, "We did not grasp the infinite but we perceive ourselves as grasped by it."[10] Also, the relationship which comes into awareness in these experiences is sensed as supremely important.[11] Although religious experiences may be few in number in a given individual life, they carry a sense of significance that exceeds the actual amount of times people have this explicit awareness. Religious experiences, therefore, bring us to awareness of a transcendent otherness which initiates contact and is supremely important.

Although religious experiences in themselves are of limited duration, they have a sustained impact in the life of the subject.[12] This impact is especially powerful if the experience is nurtured in memory and ritualized in action. There is an aftermath of the experience, a permanent residue in the subject that can be most aptly talked about as a structure of consciousness. The experience gives rise to a foundational perspective and attitude towards the total mystery of life itself. In turn, this perspective and attitude qualifies the subsequent experiences of all things within life. The perspective and attitude is characterized as religious because it forms the ultimate permeating context of the person's continuing experiences. Jonathan Edwards talks succinctly about this aftermath of religious experience:

> After this (religious experience) my sense of divine things gradually increased and became more and more lively and had more of that inward sweetness. The appearance of everything was altered. There seemed to be, as it were, a calm sweet cast or appearance of divine glory in almost everything. God's excellency, his wisdom, his purity and love seemed to appear in everything, in the sun, moon, stars, on the clouds, and blue sky, in the grass, flowers, trees, in water and all nature which used greatly to fix my mind. I often used to sit and view the moon for continuance. And in the bay spent much time viewing the clouds and skies to behold the sweet glory of God in these things. [13]

Edwards does not say he sees new things as a result of his religious experience. His testimony is that he sees old things in a new way. The result of religious experience is often a shift in perception that restructures the existing world rather than adds a whole new element to that world. [14]

Since the stylized language of Christian tradition may be too familiar and so "dead" to many, perhaps a more secular rendition of religious experience and its impact might be helpful:

> After the experience of the sense of presence I knew, as Walt Whitman expressed it, that there was more to me than was found between my hat and shoes. It was up to me to find out more about that MORE; and so, as I see it, my minuscule will was linked up with the will that our forefathers called God. I don't know what that power is, nor do I call it God. But by it I live and in my slow, often frustrated effort to learn means of communication with it I grow, inch by inch, into a person more nearly resembling a human being than was ever imagined by me to be possible. This power beyond my own ego is not altogether beyond it or separate from it. It is as personal and "of me" as the colour of my eyes, is friendly and reliable, resourceful and companionable. But on the far side of "me" it is a mystery with respect to which I put my hand on my mouth. [15]

This report catches the sense that the Mystery is both immanent and transcendent and that our relationship to it is linked to the possibility of human fulfillment.

The expressions of religiously significant experiences are as diverse as the experiences themselves. Some of them are eloquent, gripping accounts which convey the experience with such vividness and power that the listener or reader is pulled into the experience and gains a deep appreciation of what occurred. Others are stammering, roundabout reports of people whose tongue is still tied from what has happened to them. If an experience is to be more than the "private preserve" of the single individual who has been graced with it, it must find a powerful expression in language that is accessible to other people. The founders of religion are not only people who are graced with an exceptional experience of divine reality but people who are graced with the poetic gifts to articulate and convey that experience.

But, whether the expression is captivating or forgettable, an overall pattern of reporting can be discerned. The report is usually contextualized in an autobiographical or biographical narrative within which the sense of Otherness is articulated and the feelings and insights which accompanied this awareness are expressed. Often, and this is our particular concern, an image emerges within the narrative which "kernelizes" the experience. For the one articulating the experience this image seems to capture the core of what happened. As such, it functions as a code for the experience, anchors it in memory, and is the main linguistic medium through which it is shared with others.

Language is a social phenomenon before it is a personal tool. People who want to express and communicate a religious experience inevitably reach for the language which is available within the culture. This language has a particular history, and any use of it plays upon that history. This "given" of the processes of human expression presents a paradox to people who feel they have something new to say. If they are to be understood, they must use the language at hand. But, if they use the language at hand, the "novel" that they wish to express may be engulfed in the standard understanding that the language has assumed. The creative solution is to employ old language in a fresh way. Robert Funk examines this dynamic in relationship to the creative writer:

> He cannot begin with new language. He must begin with the habituated language at hand, with the language he learned at his mother's knee, but he may succeed in moving away from these sedimentations and finding his own voice. The measure of his success is commensurate with the degree to which he has infringed the semantic compact represented by the dictionary.[16]

The old language, when used in a new way, brings both recognition and surprise, continuity and discontinuity.

One of the core images for Jesus' experience of God was Abba.[17] This image sets within the overall narrative of his life, death, and resurrection and captures its internal dynamic. Schillebeeckx states this emphasis succinctly:

> The Abba experience would appear to be the source of the peculiar nature of Jesus' message and conduct, which without this religious experience, or apart from it, lose the distinctive meaning and content actually conferred on them by Jesus.[18]

It also resonates with the use of the image of God as Father in the Hebrew tradition, yet nuances it and suggests a fresh appreciation by stressing the aspects of trust and intimacy. It is for this reason that James Dunn can sum up Jesus' use of language with the the remark:

> With Jesus, in short, we see the freshness of an original mind, a new spirit, taking up old categories and concepts, remoulding them, creating them afresh, using them in a wholly new way in the light of his basic experience of God caring and commanding him and of being bound to God by the closet ties of obedience and love.[19]

Abba and the correlate Son are the images which carry the religious experience of Jesus and the experience he hoped to initiate others into.

A few remarks about how images function in relationship to religious experience will help us explore the Abba-Son experience. First, the image is not the reality. The image illumines the experience, but it does not exhaust it. It is an experience of divine reality which the image seeks to serve, and so there is always a transcendent dimension which remains unexplored. In other words, the image always breaks under the weight of what was encountered in the experience. When this is forgotten, the image no longer functions as a pathway into the mystery of God and the self. Instead, it takes up residence in the mind and links up with other ideas to form a worldview. While this in itself is not necessarily a bad move, it is not a substitute for the image as a communicator of a lived relationship. "Jesus' sense of being God's son was an existential conviction, not merely an intellectual belief."[20]

Second, the image is drawn from some aspect of the human condition in order to illumine the experience; but, also the experience is allowed to "talk back to" that aspect of the human condition which is employed. Jesus' image is taken from the metaphoric field of family life. To call God Abba is to try to experience and understand God from an analogy with the world of parenting. To use this image is to bestow an honor on family living. It is so important a part of the human scene that it can be used to understand the source of human life itself. But, what begins as a compliment often ends as a critique. For, to use the image of Abba means to draw the human world of parenting into the experience of God. In this atmosphere parenting undergoes both affirmation and critique. What is happening in the human world that is congruent with the religious experience is supported. What is happening in the human world that is out of sync with the religious experience is critiqued with the divine command to change. The flow between the world of the image and the world of the experience is two way.[21] This is the key to understanding the reason Jesus took images from the power centers of his society—the patriarchal family and the king. In that way he brought them under the experience of God and urged upon them the necessity to change.

Third, an image is open ended and, therefore, in need of further speech to express and convey the true meaning of the experience. In other words, what is the point of the comparison? Is to call God a potter to suggest that we are inert matter to be moulded as a greater power wills? Is to call God a shepherd to designate ourselves as passive sheep? To miss the point of a comparison is to end up in either humorous or disastrous understandings:

> When the psalmist tells us that a united family is like oil dripping down Aaron's beard onto the skirts of his robe, he is not trying to persuade us that the family unity is messy, greasy, or volatile; he is thinking of the all-pervasive fragrance which has so deeply impressed itself on his memory at the anointing of the high priest. (Ps. 133:2)[22]

In order to accurately express and convey the religious experience the image must be further specified by story, and the story must be held in constant tension with the felt-perception of the experience.

The image of Jesus for his experience of divine reality is not just Abba, but the Abba unfolded in many mini-stories and one major parable. It is not just "any old father," but the father who appears again and again in the conversation of Jesus and to whom his prayer and the prayer of his followers are addressed. Although father is an image that is rooted in a human experience that is common to every time and place, it cannot be interpreted in so general a fashion. It is the activities of the father who is portrayed in the gospels that give the correct content to the image. The words that this father is made to speak, the attitudes he is said to have, and the actions that we are told he delights in are the clues to what the experience is like. If we inhabit these further specifications of the image of Abba, we will arrive at the felt-perception of the experience of God. The dynamics of this felt-perception we will restate in the next section in the language of love and attempt to unravel the style of service and prayer which flow from it.

In the contemporary climate the need to relate the image of Abba to the religious experience which grounds it is particularly acute. For, in the image of God as Father many people see the distortion of the true nature of Christian faith and the source of endless oppression. The main charge, among many, is that it has been used as the ideological bolstering of patriarchal privilege. The Father God is the energizing source and validation for the second class status of women. It provides a rationality in the very nature of reality itself for the exclusion of women in certain areas of church and society and their, if you will, ontological diminishment. For many people, to call God Father is not good news but old news and bad news.

Yet, it is an undisputed fact of contemporary scholarship that the religious experience of Jesus is condensed in the word Abba. And, it is this Abba experience which not only shaped Jesus, but which Jesus made available to others and which, by extension, becomes available to every Christian as he or she enters into the community of Christ.

Robert Hamerton-Kelly has stated the dilemma succinctly:

> All theology then is caught between the fact that Jesus expressed his
> deepest experience of God by means of the symbol "Father," on the one
> hand, and the fact that some women find that symbol demeaning and
> dehumanizing on the other. This is the issue; it is a real issue. It should
> be faced in these terms, not confused or evaded.[23]

I would agree that this is certainly a major part of the problem and add
that it is not only some women who find this image dehumanizing, but
also some men. When the image functions to divide and oppress, it
would seem to have come a long way from the mouth and the mind and
the heart of the one who first gave it to us.

Our attempt will be to go through the image of Abba and its specifications to retrieve the experience which generated it. In one way this
will purge the image of its ideological mechanisms. The experience
beneath the image directly contradicts positions which stress inherent
privilege and the power to rule. But, in another way this does not solve
the pastoral question of the use of Father imagery in religious instruction and liturgy. It will only once again establish that the insidious
tendency of human nature is to use what is meant to bind us together—
the image of a universal Father—to tear us apart.

ESTABLISHED IN LOVE: THE EXPERIENCE OF ABBA

When the image of Abba is inhabited from the point of view of
affective insight, when the question we bring to the image concerns the
felt-perception of our relationship to Ultimate Mystery, the yield is
immediate. We are loved. The reality that is mediated through the
image of Abba knows what we need (Mt. 6:6), is the source of our
goodness (Mt. 5:16), gives what we ask for (Mt. 7:11), gives daily
bread and forgives (Lk. 11:3), welcomes the sinner and invites the
resentful to party (Lk. 15:11-32), does not demand ostentatious displays but sees and rewards in secret (Mt. 6:4), cares for all equally (Mt.
5:45), counts the hairs of our heads, is mindful even of the sparrows
(Mt. 10:29). These characteristics of Abba are not literal statements of
the way God acts, but cumulatively create the atmosphere of the relationship. The flow of the relationship from the side of Abba is faithful
and free love.

This central focus on love and the dimension of selfhood this love
addresses is also underlined by the account of the baptism of Jesus.
James Dunn has remarked, "Jesus' baptism by John was probably the
occasion for an experience of God which had epochal significance for
Jesus."[24] The two major metaphors of this experience are spirit and
son. In the Markan account the metaphor of son is elaborated: "You
are my Son, the Beloved; my favor rests on you" (Mk. 1:11). The

Abba-Son compact is construed as love and favor on the part of Abba. But, this is not a love and favor that are a one-time thing, not a surface showering of care. The love mediated through the image of Abba constitutes Jesus as Son. In other words, his very selfhood is established by the love he receives.

Two other symbols which circle around Jesus and attempt to interpret him direct our attention to the depth of selfhood which transcendent love hopes to address. The first is the symbol of Satan. In the gospel of Mark, Jesus is engaged in a holy war; the combatant is Satan himself. In the full-blown mythology of Satan he is a fallen angelic creature who has rebelled against the creator. His status as a fallen creature is also reflected in the Genesis story. His purpose and activity in the garden are to corrupt the creaturehood of the man and the woman, the earth dwellers. When Satan is construed as the ultimate enemy of Christ, the arena of battle is set. It is not merely the mind, heart, and actions of people that are at stake; it is the very zone of creaturehood which is the substratum of ideas, feelings, and behaviors. Christ and Satan provide twin seductions for the freedom of the creature. The ultimate self and its strivings to be free, fulfilled, and powerful are the dimensions of human life that the Abba experience seeks to influence.

This zone of creaturehood is also indicated in Paul's designation of Jesus as the New Adam. Adam is the symbol of creaturehood gone astray, creaturehood constituted in disobedience. Christ represents creaturehood in harmony with the creator. The experience that is mediated through Christ penetrates to the centered self and offers a possibility that is an alternate to the one symbolized by Satan and Adam. Whether this alternative will be seized is the initial moral dilemma of the Christian religious experience of Abba.

When transcendent love enters history, when it arrives unbidden in the life of a particular individual with a particular build-up of historical choices and asks to be received as the reality that constitutes ultimate identity, it finds "this space" already occupied. In other words, love arrives at creaturehood distorted by sin, a creaturehood which has established itself on grounds other than divine love. In the "space" which rightfully belongs to God other realities, finite and insufficient to the task of establishing creaturehood, have taken up residence. Therefore, the advent of love naturally takes the form of forgiveness for the false centering which has already occurred. This is the reason the experience Jesus made possible for people is often talked about in terms of repentance and conversion. James Mackey spells out this dynamic:

> When first there is invoked in us the experience of being valued and cherished as a gift is valued, we are already in complicity with the destruction and decay which form the ambivalence of existence. We have already grasped at possessions or power for our security, thrown up

the barriers, and sown the seeds of hatred, if we have not actually deprived others of the means of subsistence, or maimed or killed. We are already guilty, and to the guilty the sense of being valued and cherished and accepted comes across necessarily as a sense of being forgiven.[25]

Put somewhat enigmatically, the arrival of free and undeserved love always finds us undeserving—and that was the last thing we thought we were. It then dawns on us that all the "deserving" things about us really functioned as weapons of oppression to establish ourselves over-against our brothers and sisters. It is at this moment that love turns to forgiveness.

The conversion experience which is initiated by the arrival of transcendent love can be characterized as having four moments. First, there is the uncovering of the zone of creaturehood, the surfacing of the ultimate self which is the buried energy of attitude and action. Second, there is the recognition that this selfhood has been constituted wrongfully. Our creaturehood has been freely appropriated by us in a destructive way. Third, there is a need to surrender to the love that has been experienced and allow it to constitute our selfhood. Fourth, there are the new possibilities of life which emerge if this conversion process is engaged in. Throughout these moments freedom is always operative. We can abort the process, play with it, give ourselves to it in a stinting fashion, or embrace it wholeheartedly. The advent of love as a gift and our strange reception that combines welcome and resistance are what we want to explore.

First, there needs to be an uncovering. When we are considering religious experience, what we see is not what we get. What we see are language and actions. But, beneath the tumultuous surface there are a hidden integration, a source of energy and direction, a fundamental orientation of the self within the Mystery of life. This centered self provides the assumptions out of which we live. We seldom investigate these foundational assumptions explicitly. We take them for granted. "That is the way life is," we say deep inside ourselves, "and therefore we are who we are." It is precisely this centered self and the assumptive world it generates that the Abba experience mediated by Jesus invades.

This hidden yet powerful dimension of human reality enters awareness when it explicitly contradicted. One of the ways Jesus employed to surface the centered self and its assumptive world was to tell stories which reversed the normal expectations. A story about a Samaritan who helps a Jew, about a man who works only an hour but gets a full day's pay, about a righteous man whose prayer is not heard and a sinner who has the ear of God, about the poor who will inherit the Kingdom and the rich who will be turned away empty, about a man who turns the other cheek, and many more. The result of hearing these stories was imaginative shock. They contradicted "the way life is," and so brought to mind and heart what was taken for granted and accepted as normal. The zone of creaturehood and the way creature-hood was construed were uncovered. Once uncovered, it could become the object of investigation, and possibly change could come about.

The Abba experience which constituted Jesus' selfhood and which he mediated to other people contained a profound contradiction to a central assumption of the centered self. Perhaps the best way to understand this assumption is to look at the structure of conversion which was standard in the Judaism of Jesus' day. The procedure was that the sinner was converted first and then became part of the community. Conversion first, communion second. "The novum in the act of Jesus was to reverse this structure: communion first, conversion second."[26] The Abba experience connotes a love that accepts us just because we are creatures, previous to our efforts to prove ourselves worthy and in spite of our failures that prove we are not worthy. As James Mackey puts it, this type forgiving love "had nothing to do with previous acts of contrition or promises of penance, much less with penance actually performed or sacrifices already made. It was the sense of our acceptance by God, not despite what we were, or because of what we were, but as we were."[27]

We are not used to this. Upfront and unconditional love is not the "way the world works." We are trained in cautious and limited acceptance of ourselves and others. We know there are "things that make us good" and "things that make us bad." If we parade the good before others and bury the bad, we have a good chance of finding acceptance. On the other hand, if we are known by all to be bad and the very structure of society ratifies this judgment, then we can be assured of systematic rejection. What we do not expect is a love that cuts through these rather clear and common sense regulations to embrace us at a level deeper than human thought and action. When this happens (as it does in the Abba experience), the assumptions of the centered self about what makes it worthy are uncovered and called into question.

The first moment after the inrush of unconditional love is the awareness of the centered self or, in traditional language, the soul. The second moment is the recognition that we have attempted to establish this self in ways that are both self-defeating for us and oppressive for others. Sebastian Moore says that he can think of only one experience that is universal to the human race. Everyone wants to be desired by that which he/she desires. We want to be loved by that which we love. And, what we love most of all is life itself. So, we are continually asking of the Mystery of life: am I significant in your eyes? This is the human race's preconscious love affair with God which is built into the structure of finitude. When no answer arrives to this unrelenting question, we begin a series of antics to make ourselves attractive to the Mystery we so deeply desire. But, the more we try to make ourselves loveable, the deeper the quandary becomes. We are living out an experience which F. Scott Fitzgerald called the horror "of trying to please and not being able."

Unconvinced that our deepest selves are grounded by a transcendent love, we conjure up love substitutes. We establish ourselves in terms of wealth, power, goodness, fame, and talent. Our possessions of these things make us worthy, and without them we fall back into the terrible question that does not seem to have an answer. With them we reenforce our desirability. We flaunt what we have, answering the question of creaturehood with the bluster: "How can I not be loveable when I am so wealthy, powerful, good, famous, and talented?"

Yet, in the gospels, wealth, righteousness, and prestigious power are the main obstacles to receiving the Abba experience. The reason is that there is no room for divine love when we have established our creaturehood on other grounds. Divine love is not needed when a love substitute has been found and embraced. On the other hand, the Abba experience is received by the poor, the sinner, and the lowly precisely because they do not have available to them the finite surrogates. They can allow themselves to be loved for no other reason than the fact that they are and to rejoice in a love that is so gracious. This is one of the reasons scholars talk about a hermeneutic privilege of the poor. They understand that they must be established from outside themselves by a reality which desires them out of its own abundance and not because of their boasting. This is also the reason the Kingdom is received by the child. The child is vulnerable, and his or her worth is constituted, not by strenuous achievement, but by the love of the parent. We are not talking about passivity but about an initial receptivity which will eventuate in creative action.

This, of course, is the ancient question of idolatry, mistaking the finite for the infinite and placing our hopes in it. As Ernst Käsemann has suggested, Jesus is a Jew of the first commandment.[28] He has no other gods before the only God. This experience of the primacy of divine love is embodied in the images and stories of Jesus and has had insightful translations in the theologies of Paul, Augustine, Luther, and Tillich, to name a few. But, the recognition that occurs when unconditional love enters is not only that we have attempted a false grounding. What dawns on us is that this false grounding has had disastrous effects on ourselves and those we have dealt with. It is this awareness that makes the primary characteristic of this love forgiveness.

When we ground our creaturehood falsely in some finite reality, we begin a process of anxious striving and self-deception. If it is wealth that attempts to confer self worth, we notice that we never have enough. The certain amount we thought would satisfy us never does. We need more; but, as we acquire it, even more looms before us. Our infinite appetite devours every finite appeasement. The promise that money holds out to us it cannot fulfill. Our idol "makes us grasp more eagerly and tear more savagely at the things we think can give us the life we want, and, as we do so, feel more utterly the futility, and fear more persistently the hopelessness of it all."[29] We live a life of anxious and hopeless striving. It is to this inherently destructive posture of chronic worry that Jesus offered an alternative in his beautiful meditation on the birds of the air and the lilies of the field (Lk. 12:22-32).

If we establish our creaturehood in righteousness, a subtle process of self-deception is initiated which often culminates in a life of outright lie which the gospels label hypocrisy.[30] When our goodness constitutes our self worth, we do not dare do wrong. Wrong threatens the very essence of who we are. Yet, inevitably we do do wrong. Sin runs deep in us and breaks out in ways we do not expect. The generous deed is done for self-serving motives. We are silent in the face of unjust systems. Yet, we cannot admit to any wrongdoing, for it would threaten our self worth. So, we protect our core self by denying the wrongs we do. We hide from the light and rationalize away the evil we are involved in. Soon our perceptions are so distorted that a gnat and a camel swim in the cup of wine we drink; we strain the gnat and swallow down the camel whole.

But, the most devastating result of false grounding is not what it does to the idolater, but how it affects other people. The only real way that we know we are worthy is if other people are not. If wealth is the core of our selfhood, other people must be poor to reenforce us. If it is goodness, other people must be designated sinners to reenforce us. If it is prestige, other people must be downtrodden to reenforce us. In other words, if we are not grounded in a universal and transcendent love, we have built division into the essence of who we are. All our efforts to build ourselves up, therefore, mean that other people are automatically put down. When the petitioner asked Jesus to make his brother give him his rightful share of the inheritance, Jesus' angry reply was, "O Man, who made me a judge or divider over you?" (Lk. 12:13). Creaturehood which is not freely rooted in the creator is inherently oppressive.

With the arrival of transcendent love comes the awareness that the ultimate self has been destructively grounded, that a life of anxious striving, self-deception, and oppression has been the normal course. We now know ourselves as sinners. We know this only because love has revealed this to us, not for the purpose of condemnation, but for the purpose of conversion. We tend toward despair and, as the runaway younger son, characterize ourself as a hired hand. We have lost true sonship and daughtership. We need a love which now will love us more than we love ourselves. The Abba experience contains this love. The same love whose initial contact convicted us of sin does not abandon us. This love is faithful to us in our alienation from it. It waits on the hill and runs to meet us with kisses of welcome. This faithful love permits us to forgive ourselves and seek forgiveness of others. All it asks is that we surrender to it.

The third moment of the Abba experience is that we must let go and allow God to secure our creaturehood in divine love. This means we must abandon not only the surrogate groundings of our self-worth but also the self-hatred that we might be wallowing in as a result of our encounter with unconditional Love. The returning son in Jesus' parable must allow the Father to dress him in the clothes of sonship. At the moment he cannot dress himself. He would rather remain a hired hand. But, the same love that convicts us of distortion also convicts us of beauty. He will be received as son even though he himself cannot find enough confidence to claim it. This act of surrender becomes the ultimate paradox. The very self-worth we wish to claim as a strenuous achievement we must accept as a gift from beyond ourselves.

William James has stated that "self-surrender has been and always must be regarded as the vital turning-point of the religious life."[31] E.D. Starbuck explores this moment insightfully:

> He must relax, that is, he must fall back on the larger Power that makes for righteousness, which has been welling up in his own being, and let it finish in its own way the work it has begun. . . . The act of yielding, in this point of view, is giving one's self over to the new life, making it the center of a new personality, and living, from within, the truth of it which had before been viewed objectively.[32]

The act of surrendering, then, is really a process of re-centering, a free acceptance of ourselves as reconstituted by a larger Power.

The content of what we give up is not lost. The finite realities that we have foisted into the role of God are part of the good creation. They need not be jettisoned. The source of distortion is our appropriation of the good creation. We have turned it, through grasping, into what it is not. The Christian formulation of the enigma of human sinfulness is not: what things are good and what things are bad, but how do good things go bad? With this understanding, what we surrender comes back to us—not as substitutes for divine love, but as part of creation which is meant for enjoyment and transformation. Another paradox of the paradox haunted Abba experience emerges. That which is given up returns a hundredfold: the one who loses life, finds it. This dynamic found new formulation in the classic lines from Francis Thompson's *The Hound of Heaven:*

> All which I took from thee I did but take,
>   Not for thy harms,
> But just that thou might'st seek it in My arms.
>   All which thy child's mistake
> Fancies as lost, I have stored for thee at home:
>   Rise, clasp My hand, and come![33]

In this articulation the Abba experience finds a complementary image. It is the experience of finding a home in which nothing is lost, but all things are rearranged, finding their proper place.

The moment of surrender unfolds into new possibilities. The experience will gradually insinuate itself into interpersonal and social life. We will explore two outcomes of the experience—the freedom to serve and the passion to pray. But, before we do this, we should make concrete this experience of divine love in a story. This is the story of Peter and Jesus and the miraculous catch of fish:

> It is known by everyone who cares to know that the Lord Jesus and St. Peter used to repair to the local tavern after a hard day of ministry to break bread and drink wine together.
>
> On a certain rainy night after St. Peter had had a few beers, he turned to the Lord Jesus and grinned, "We're doing real good."
>
> "We?," said the Lord Jesus.
>
> Peter was silent. "All right, you're doing real good," he finally said.
>
> "Me?," said the Lord Jesus.
>
> Peter was silent a second time. "All right, God's doing real good," he reluctantly admitted.
>
> The Lord Jesus laughed and hit the table with glee.
>
> It was the laugh that got to St. Peter. He pushed his face toward Jesus and blurted out, "Look it! I was somebody before you came along. You didn't make me. I know now everybody says, 'There goes the Lord Jesus and his sidekick St. Peter. Jesus cures the sick and Peter helps them up.' But it wasn't always that way. People knew me in my own right. They would say, 'There goes Peter, the greatest fisherman in all of Galilee.' I was respected and looked up to."
>
> "I heard that you were a very good fisherman, Peter," said the Lord Jesus.
>
> "You're damn right I was. And tomorrow I am going to prove it. We are going to go fishing and you will see how the other fishermen respect me and look to my lead."
>
> "I would love to go fishing, Peter. I have never been fishing," said the Lord Jesus who was always looking for new adventures. "But what will we do with all the fish we are going to catch?"
>
> "Store them up. Eat them one day at a time. Wait till there is a shortage, then put them on the market at top dollar and turn a big profit. Many things." Peter smiled the smile of the fox.
>
> "Oh!," said the Lord Jesus, who had that puzzled and pained look on his face that Peter had often observed—as if something that had never crossed his mind just made a forced entry. Peter wondered how someone as obviously intelligent as Jesus could be so slow in some matters.
>
> So the next morning at dawn the Lord Jesus and St. Peter were down at the shore readying their boat. And it was just as St. Peter had said. When the other fishermen saw St. Peter, they sidled over. "Going out, Peter?," they asked.

"Yes," answered Peter, not looking up from the nets.

"Mind if we follow along?"

"Why not?," shrugged Peter. And he looked at the Lord Jesus and said, "See!"

St. Peter's boat led the way. The Lord Jesus was in the prow hanging on tightly for he was deeply afraid of the water. Now St. Peter was a scientist of a fisherman. He tasted the water, scanned the sky, peered down into the lake—and gave the word in a whisper, "Over there."

"Why isn't anyone talking?," asked the Lord Jesus.

"Shhhh!," Peter shook his head.

The boats formed a wide circle around the area that Peter had pointed out. "Let down the nets," Peter's voice crept over the surface of the water.

"Why don't they just toss them in?," asked the Lord Jesus, who had hopes of learning about fishing.

A second "shhhh!" came from St. Peter.

The fishermen let down their nets and began to pull them in. But something was wrong. The muscles of their arms did not tighten under the weight of fish. The nets rose quickly, the arms of the men slack. All they caught was water.

The fishermen rowed their boats over to St. Peter. "The greatest fisherman in all of Galilee, my grandmother's bald head. You brought us all the way out here for nothing. We have wasted the best hours of the day and have not one fish to show for it. Stick to preaching, Peter." And they rowed toward shore, shouting over their shoulder at Peter.

The Lord Jesus said nothing.

St. Peter checked the nets. He tasted the sea a second time. He scanned the sky a second time. He looked at the Lord Jesus a second time and said, "Over there!"

No sooner had he said, "Over there!," then the Lord Jesus was at the oars, rowing mightily.

And all day long under the searing sun the Lord Jesus and St. Peter rowed from place to place on the sea of Galilee. And all day long under the searing sun the Lord Jesus and St. Peter let down their nets. And all day long under the searing sun the Lord Jesus and St. Peter hauled in their nets. And all day long under the searing sun the Lord Jesus and St. Peter caught nothing.

Evening fell and an exhausted St. Peter raised the sail to make for shore. The weary Lord Jesus held on tightly in the prow.

It was then, as the boat glided toward shore, that all the fish in the sea of Galilee came to the surface. They leapt on one side of the boat and they leapt on the other side of the boat. They leapt behind the boat and they leapt in front of the boat. They formed a cordon around the boat, escorting it toward shore in full fanfare.

And then in a mass suicide of fish, they leapt into the boat, landing in the laughing lap of the Lord Jesus, smacking the astonished St. Peter in the face. When the boat arrived at shore, it was brimming, creaking, sinking under the weight of fish.

The other fishermen were waiting. They gathered around St. Peter and slapped him on the back. "Peter, you scoundrel. You knew where the fish were all the time and never let on." They hit him on the shoulder. "Peter, you rogue. You put us on. You surely are the greatest fisherman in all of Galilee."

But Peter was uncharacteristically silent. He only said, "Give the fish to everyone. Tonight, no home in this village will go without food." After that, he said nothing.

But later in the tavern Peter stared at the table and spoke in a chastened voice to Jesus. "Go away from me, I am a sinful man. I wanted to use my skills to dominate others, to show them I was better than they were, to keep them in their place. I did not want the fish to feed hunger but to lord it over you and the others, to make things better for me and worse for everyone else. You better go away from me."

At that moment Jesus loved Peter with the love that moves the sun and stars; and he had no intention of going away. There was more fishing to be done.

THE FREEDOM TO SERVE

One of the consequences of the Abba experience is a new understanding and practice of power. When the self has been recreated on new grounds, it sees and acts in the world in a new way. This naturally causes conflict. Perfect behavior appears as perfect only in a perfect environment. When the environment is distorted by a destructive appropriation of the fundamental fact of finitude, behavior that flows from a creative appropriation of finitude appears as strange and, to those who benefit from the established style of behavior, dangerous. Therefore, one of the more fascinating ways to trace the "power as service" themes of the Abba experience is to link together the conflicts which Jesus had with his disciples. Many of them are about the use of power, how the Abba experience is to be worked out in interpersonal and social life.

One of the problems the religious authorities of Jesus' times had with him is that he claimed to forgive sins (Mk. 2:1-12). He arrogated to himself power that was proper to God. We have reinterpreted the code phrase, "forgiveness of sins," as the communication of divine love which provides a new grounding for created selfhood. But, what was even more radical than Jesus' claim to be the mediator of divine love was the fact he passed that power along. In fact, it seems the essence of the Abba experience is that it be communicated to others. The story of the forgiven servant who, in turn, does not forgive is a tragic tale of distortion (Mt. 18:23-35). The vision which grows out the experience seems to be an endless chain of mediation—through Jesus to the disciples, through the disciples to others, through those others to others still, and on and on. This is what some have called the contagion of Christian faith.

One of the classic scenes of the handing on of power is Peter's confession of faith in Matthew 16:13-20. Peter recognizes the source of Jesus' power is his appropriation of true created Sonship, and is rewarded for this understanding, which is credited, not to himself, but to God's gift, with the keys to the kingdom. Peter and, by implication, the others now have the power which accrues to the Abba experience. Further episodes will reveal the true nature of that power.

The very next episode in the gospel of Matthew (16:21-23) records a conflict between Jesus and Peter. The content of the conflict is the nature and use of power. Jesus predicts that he will go up to Jerusalem where he will be put to death and rise on the third day. Peter will have none of it. "Heaven preserve you, Lord. This must not happen to you." For this sincere display of concern Peter is called Satan and told to get back into the following of Jesus, to allow Jesus to show the way. What is happening in this cryptic interchange?

Peter knows that Jesus is the Son of Power, and he knows the way power works. Power is for the purpose of exempting yourself from the fate which the powerless have to undergo. The sons of kings never die in the wars their fathers start. The daughters of legislators are never ground up in the tax laws their mothers enact. Those in power use it to secure themselves against the factors which would diminish them. In this context it is certainly folly for the Son of Ultimate Power to submit to the conditions of powerlessness. But, Jesus is redefining the understanding and use of power. Power embraces the conditions of life in a new way; it does not exempt itself. The power that flows from divine love is not armor but increased vulnerability, an openness to life which will overcome its destructiveness by undergoing it.

A second episode which contains a conflict about power is Matthew 18:21-22. Peter, knowing that Jesus is forgiveness prone, offers a generous estimate of how many times our brothers and sisters should be forgiven. "As often as seven times?" In this interchange his rebuke is milder but just as undercutting. "Not seven, I tell you, but seventy-times seven." There is more here than just the contrast between a definite number and an infinite capacity. Peter has the keys, and what good are keys unless you can lock some people in and others out. Power knows itself as power only when it excludes. Until it excommunicates, it is never sure that it is communicating. Peter is subtly asking when he can exercise his power and exclude. Jesus' rejoinder is questioning his assumption. Power is not for the purposes of exclusion. It is for the mission of inclusion. The power that flows from the Abba experience brings people together; it does not tear them apart.

A third episode, and the most famous conflict between Jesus and Peter, is recorded in the thirteenth chapter of the gospel of John. Jesus is washing the feet of the disciples. Peter refuses this service. Jesus says that if Peter does not allow himself to be washed, he will have nothing in common with him. The impetuous Peter then requests an entire bath. The disconcerting factor in the story is initially that the master has become the servant. And, the lesson is not lost on Peter. If Jesus, who is the master, acts like this, what does it say about Peter's use of his authority and power. Peter's reluctance would seem to stem from the fact that this feet washing is a prophecy for his own life.

But, the issue of power in the story goes beyond the mere fact of reversal. It is what Jesus has chosen to serve that is the core of Peter's balking. The master serves concrete human needs. Dirty feet are the objects of his ministrations. But, the rhetoric of service which abounds in the Christian church is often more noble than this. Service is given to the Kingdom, the idealized social order, the vision of the future. And, when this is what is served, a crushed body is tolerated, a mangled spirit is surely an acceptable price. The Abba experience not only demands that power serve but demands that it serve concrete human need.

Two short episodes in Luke (9:49-50; 9:51-56) further specify the use of power. John tells Jesus that the disciples met a man who was casting out devils in his name, and they told him to stop. The reason that they urged the man to stop was that "he was not one of us." Jesus' response was, "You must not stop him. Anyone who is not against you is for you." Power often wants to stop goodness if it cannot get anything out of it. It wants to control the good. If it cannot be attributed to our group, then it must be stopped. The bolstering of the group takes precedence over salvific action. The fact that now there lives a person free of demons is insignificant. The matter of importance is that we have not worked this wonder. This tendency to usurp the good and to deny it where it cannot be usurped is a distortion of the overflowing power of the Abba experience.

The disciples went ahead to make preparations in a Samaritan village. The Samaritans would not receive them. James and John suggested to Jesus that he call down fire from heaven and burn them up. Jesus suggested that they find another village. The tendency of power is to use it for revenge. If we have been rejected, reject back— only harder. Lack of hospitality is met by cremation. The way of power is retribution. The disciples know this, but Jesus knows something different. Power is invitation to new life; and when it is rejected, it seeks other opportunities. The preoccupation of power is not violence but creative invitation.

The consequence of experiencing God as Abba and ourselves as daughters and sons of Love is the freedom to serve. Since we have ultimately grounded ourselves in God and not in our own efforts, our powers are redirected. They are creatively released for "Kingdom" activity. This means that we do not use power to exempt ourselves from the conditions of life but to embrace those conditions in an effort to transform them; that we do not use power to exclude but to include; that we do not dedicate our talents to the service of abstract ideals but to real human needs; that we use our authority to allow the good to flourish and not to coopt it; that we use whatever position we have to create opportunities and not to avenge ourselves on others. Once human power has been regrounded in divine love, it has a radically different agenda.

Out of the Abba experience and with this renewed understanding of power we confront the ongoing situations of our lives. These reflections do not tell what we are to do. In the first analysis it is not a blueprint for the Christian use of parental, educational, ecclesiastical, and political power. But, it does point out our deep seated tendency to use power in a ego-serving and oppressive way. It also touches on the general attitudes which must guide all exercise of power that hopes to be salvific. The actual embodying of these attitudes in diverse situations demands creativity and ingenuity. It always entails a process of evaluation and redoing. What energizes this endless effort to purge our power of distortion and make it serve human solidarity and well-being is the Abba experience itself, the awareness of an empowering Love that flows from the transcendent Mystery which encompasses all creation.

THE PASSION TO PRAY

Before Jesus was an advocate of prayer, he was its most thoroughgoing critic.[34] He mocked the prayer of the righteous with its pompous boasting before God. "Thank God I am not like the rest of men" (Lk. 18:11). He brutally uncovered the real reason behind the public display of prayer—self-advertisement (Mt. 6:5). He outrageously linked outward piety with acts of injustice. "Beware . . . men who swallow the property of widows, while making a show of lengthy prayers" (Mk. 12:40). He attacked the core assumption of all professional pray-ers that more is better. "In your prayers do not babble as the pagans do, for they think that by using many words they will make themselves heard" (Mt. 6:7-8). Finally, and most scathingly, he took up the ancient prophetic denunciation of substituting prayer for just action. "It is not those who say to me, 'Lord, Lord,' who will enter the Kingdom of Heaven, but the person who does the will of my Father in Heaven" (Mt. 7:21). In the light of this consistent critique, it is not an idle question that one of his disciples asks, "Lord, teach us to pray" (Lk. 11:1).

The reason that Jesus so vigorously attacked the prayer practices of his day was that they contradicted the Abba experience. The prayer practices show frightened and panicky people before an all powerful presence they cannot be sure of. These people alternately boast and babble, doing anything to get the attention of a God who is basically bored with them. Their prayer is just one more strategy in the overall campaign of ego glorification. To pray in public for attention and rip off widows for security are perfectly compatible. Both flow from the shaken self, desperately grasping for something to hold on to. In short, these prayers are not a response to the inrush of divine love but a sign of the stubborn resistance to accept our lives as given from beyond ourselves.

What are the appropriate purpose, practice, and content of prayer that flows from the Abba experience? Most basically, prayer cultivates the relationship which was established in the Abba experience. The initial salvific contact of God and humankind, mediated through Jesus and expressed as Abba, needs time to develop. Its implications are not fully grasped in the first flush of the experience. The most cherished analogy for prayer is a dialogue between two people who love each another; and it is a helpful way to explore this situation. In the first meeting all the lovers know is fascination, and that their individual lives are "saved" when they are together and "lost" when they are apart. With more encounters come greater intimacy and a deepened appreciation of what their mutual love is accomplishing in them. There also develops a sense of responsibility to their love. They become aware of the conditions under which it will grow and the conditions under which it will atrophy. The purpose of prayer is to deepen, appropriate, and become more responsible to the experience of divine love.

There are a few constant characteristics in the prayer that is generated by the Abba experience and seeks to keep it alive. Certain perceptions and feelings gradually establish themselves as central. Qualities of the relationship begin to emerge. These qualities provide the ongoing atmosphere of prayer time and prayer space. Whatever the particular content of prayer might be, these factors are present and influential. We will investigate three.

First, the divine and the human are inseparably linked, and the bonds between people strengthened. The first line of the Lord's prayer is, "Our Father in heaven." Although prayer may be an action of the solitary self, it always addresses the reality that binds people together. The opening word must be "our." If it is not, we are in danger of creating a private God, one who looks after us but is neglectful of others. Prayer would then foster division because some would have the ear of God and some would not. But, the God encountered in Christian prayer is the grounding of human solidarity. The divine love that is dialogued with talks to more than me; and so through it, I am related to all others. As the poetess Anne Sexton put it: "To pray, Jesus knew, is to be a man carrying a man."

Although the Father is characterized as in heaven and so transcendent to the affairs of earth, the very fact that we can say Father indicates divine presence. The portrait is definitely different from the Oriental Potentate God who lives in the sky and can be contacted only through the bribes of slaughtered cattle and burnt wheat. The God of Jesus' prayer has already made contact, and his contact has brought life, and so he is called Father. The life that has been given comes from beyond ourselves, from an Otherness that is the source of all created reality, and so we say "in heaven." But, the perception is clear. The divine and the human are not alienated, but in intimate communion.

This interaction of the divine and the human is considerably deepened in the "forgiveness" section of the Lord's Prayer. This petition seems to say that the proper response to the experience of divine love is to transform it into human love toward one another. The energy and inspiration of this human love will be perceived as divine. "Your light must shine in the sight of men, so that, seeing your good works, they may give the praise to your Father in heaven" (Mt. 5:16). If we have been forgiven, we are to forgive in turn. When we do this, we do more than merely "give as we have received." In the act of loving others we enter more deeply into our own experience of divine love. As Norman Perrin puts it: "In the context of God's forgiveness men learn to forgive, and in the exercise of forgiveness toward their fellow man they enter ever more deeply into an experience of the divine forgiveness."[35] The atmosphere of the prayer which passionately pursues the Abba experience is the intimate bonding of God, self, and neighbor.

A second quality of the prayer that cultivates the Abba experience is that it is other-centered and strategic. After the initial address in the Lord's Prayer, the priorities are set out. "Your name be held holy; your Kingdom come; your will be done, on earth as in heaven." The concerns are not those of the one praying; they are those of the one prayed to. The one praying has experienced love and expressed it as "Our Father." The response to this love is to espouse the concerns of the Lover. This is the true maturity of prayer. Prayer is not the soliciting of the Last Power of Human Life to do our bidding, a begging of God to do for us what we cannot do for ourselves. This procedure, all too common in prayer, subtly places us at the center of the universe and reverses the creature-creator relationship. Prayer is for the purpose of discerning the cause of God in human life and marshalling our energies to serve it.

This other-centered quality of prayer provides a new image for the God of the dialogue. This image can be seen in the two stories of Jesus that are usually cited as examples of perseverance in prayer—the unjust judge and the friend at midnight. The judge does not give the widow her due at first, but because she is relentless in her request, he gives in. The friend does not gain entry into the house at first, but because he will not stop knocking, the householder finally opens the door and gives him the food he wishes. The point seems to be persistence. God is somewhat like an unjust judge and a sleepy householder, but our never-ceasing prayers will eventually turn him just and welcoming.

An alternate interpretation, leaning heavily on the prophetic tradition, identifies the cause of God with the widow and the friend outside and ourselves with the unjust judge and the reluctant homeowner. This interpretation reverses our understanding of prayer. Prayer is not the verbal entreaty of a reluctant God, but the way we relate and respond to a pursuing God. God is the widow, and if we will not give justice for the sake of justice, she will nag us until we give it out of embarrassment. God is the friend outside, and if we will not give bread out of friendship, he will knock until we give it out of annoyance. These parables are about prayer, but not how we petition God. They are about God's petitioning us to respond to the oppressed and the outcast.

In prayer we lay ourselves open to the cause of God. Nikos Kazantzakis opens his autobiography, *Report to Greco,* with three prayers. "Three kinds of souls, three prayers: 1. I am a bow in your hands, Lord. Draw me, lest I rot. 2. Do not overdraw me, Lord. I shall break. 3. Overdraw me, Lord, and who cares if I break." In prayer we become available for the divine mission. We must be careful of this. It easily turns to fanaticism. The only check is the reminder that the divine cause is love.

Prayer, then, is for plotting. In the overall story of Jesus the rhythm of prayer and action is firmly established. Jesus prays at times of important decisions—when he chooses the twelve, when he sets his face toward Jerusalem, when the influential and powerful decide against him, when he faces the possibilities of suffering, when death finally comes. In the middle of a whirlwind ministry and in the face of growing opposition Jesus retires to desert places to pray. The implication is that the path of love is not all that easily discerned. And, if prayer does not complement action, action will go its own way, breaking loose from the Abba experience and inevitably betraying it. Nowhere is this more evident than in the Gethsemane prayer: "Abba! Everything is possible for you. Take this cup away from me. But let it be as You, not I, would have it" (Mk. 14:36). In prayer we gauge our situation and project the path that will most serve God's cause.

This fact that prayer is other-centered and strategic means that it can never be divorced from experience and action. On the one hand, prayer flows out of the Abba experience we have undergone. It is meditation on the implications of that experience and the cultivation of the relationship which was established at that time. On the other hand, prayer looks to the further embodiment of that experience. It envisions actions that will be congruent with it. Any type of prayer that does not stem from experience or has no overflow into action is too isolationist. Prayer may provide times of ecstasy; but, as long as that ecstasy is experienced by people in the throes of sin and grace, it cannot be an end itself. The touch of God always means personal and social transformation.

There is another aspect about a style of prayer that gives the pray-er over to the cause of God. Within the Lord's Prayer there is a terrible realism. It is embodied in the phrase, "Lead us not into temptation but deliver us from evil." People who live out of the love of God will cause deep offense. While their lives will be an invitation to many, they will also be an intolerable effrontery to others. Persecution will inevitably come. Prayer foresees this and strengthens the pray-ers for a future which will include sacrifice and suffering. We firm up our resolve and pray to be faithful to the Abba experience when we are put to the test. Fidelity to the experience of God, no matter what the cost, is the last whisper of the Lord's prayer. James Mackey explores this fidelity:

> Life itself, and everything that became part of that life, he (Jesus) held as a grace, as one holds a precious gift, gently, as one holds a soft, delicate thread which, as it is drawn back will, if one does not pull at it and break it, draw one to its very source . . . When force was brought to bear on him, inevitably, in order to make him divide and grasp like the rest, then, in final witness to the faith by which he lived and by which alone life is served, he refused to do so. He held the thread as gently as ever, as it was drawn back, and in doing so he deprived death of its sting, robbed it of its only victory. Death's victory over us is to enslave us in fear, to make us grasp more eagerly and tear more savagely at the things we think can give us the life we want, and, as we do so, feel more utterly the futility, and fear more persistently the hopelessness of it all. Jesus denied death that victory.[36]

Prayer envisions a test and begins the process of resourcing ourselves so that we will undergo it with fidelity.

The third constant quality of praying out of the Abba experience has to do with the affective flow of the relationship. The bonding of God, self, and neighbor and the other-centered, strategic nature of prayer are the deepened awareness and mental activity of prayer. But, prayer is language of the heart. It is impassioned conversation that includes praise and gratitude. The overriding feeling of prayer is that we are nurtured by God. "Give us this day our daily bread." This metaphoric expression means that God is the source of our life and that he will sustain it. This confidence gives us the power to engage in the task. Only the rooted risk. Since we receive our lives daily from the abundance of God, we can embrace life without fear. In prayer we come into contact with this life giving reality.

It is difficult to get at this dimension of prayer. It is the quality of trust, intimacy, warmth, delight, of sheer exuberance at the love that suffuses the one who prays. For this quality we must turn to the poets. Perhaps something from the Psalms would be appropriate. But, a modern poem comes to mind:

> I'm mooring my rowboat
> at the dock of the island called God.
> This dock is made in the shape of a fish
> and there are many boats moored
> at many different docks.
> "It's okay," I say to myself,

with blisters that broke and healed
and broke and healed—
saving themselves over and over.
And salt sticking to my face and arms like
a glue-skin pocked with grains of tapioca.
I empty myself from my wooden boat
and onto the flesh of The Island.

"On with it!" He says and thus
we squat on the rocks by the sea
and play—can it be—
a game of poker.
He calls me.
I win because I hold a royal straight flush.
He wins because He holds five aces.
A wild card had been announced
but I had not heard it
being in such a state of awe
when He took out the cards and dealt.
As he plunks down His five aces
and I sit grinning at my royal flush,
He starts to laugh,
the laughter rolling like a hoop out of His mouth
and into mine,
and such laughter that He doubles right over me
laughing a Rejoice-Chorus at our two triumphs.
Then I laugh, the fishy dock laughs
the sea laughs. The Island laughs.
The Absurd laughs.

Dearest dealer,
I with my royal straight flush,
love you so for your wild card,
that untamable, eternal, gut-driven *ha-ha*
and lucky love.[37]

The experience of prayer that flows from the Abba encounter and holds together God and people and commits the pray-er to God's cause feels like that.

CONCLUSION

The Christian tradition remembers Jesus. We do so because he inaugurated an experience of the ultimate Mystery of life which generations of people have hailed as salvific. In the retelling of his story we enter into the possibility of experiencing this salvation. One of Jesus' main images for this experience was Abba. The Abba experience was the free inrush of divine love which restructured the foundations of selfhood. Since this restructuring happens in a world where the self is structured falsely, the experience entails forgiveness and repentance. The touch of Abba exposes the hidden self, convicts it of sin, and solicits it to surrender to the new life of divine love. The outcome of this experience is a life of service and prayer. The style of service reverses the dominant tendency to use power to establish ourselves over-against our brothers and sisters. The style of prayer reverses the isolationist, ego centered, unfeeling pleas to a Higher Power approach. We now serve in a way that empowers and gives life; and pray in a way that unites and transforms.

NOTES

[1] Cf. Larry Shinn, *Two Sacred Worlds* (Nashville: Abingdon, 1977), Chapter Three.

[2] Cf. Peter Slater, *The Dynamics of Religion: Meaning and Change in Religious Traditions* (New York: Harper & Row, 1978).

[3] Cf. Edward Schillebeeckx, *Interim Report on the Books Jesus & Christ* (New York: Crossroad, 1981), Chapter Two.

[4] The classic is William James, *The Varieties of Religious Experience* (New York: New American Library, 1958). Two other helpful works are Richard Woods, ed., *Understanding Mysticism* (New York: Doubleday, 1981), and Sir Alister Hardy, *The Spiritual Nature of Man* (Oxford: Clarendon Press, 1979).

[5] Cf. Shinn, Chapter One.

[6] Cf. Charles Meyer, *The Touch of God* (New York: Alba House, 1971).

[7] Cf. Charles Davis, *Body as Spirit: The Nature of Religious Feeling* (New York: The Seabury Press, 1976).

[8] Cf. John Shea, *Stories of Faith* (Chicago: Thomas More Press, 1980), Chapter One.

[9] Cf. Gordon Kaufman, *Systematic Theology: A Historicist Perspective* (New York: Charles Scribner's Sons, 1968), Chapter Two.

[10] Paul Tillich, *Dynamics of Faith* (New York: Harper, 1957).

[11] Cf. F. David Martin, *Art and the Religious Experience: The "Language" of the Sacred* (Lewisburg: Bucknell University Press, 1972), Chapter One.

[12] Cf. Walter Gulick, "Archetypal Experiences," *Soundings,* Fall, 1981.

[13] Quoted in James W. Jones, "Reflections on the Problem of Religious Experience," *Philosophy of Religion and Theology* (Published by The American Academy of Religion, 1971).

[14] Cf. C. Daniel Batson, J. Christian Beker, and W. Malcolm Clark, *Commitment without Ideology* (Philadelphia: United Church Press), Chapters Two and Three.

[15] Quoted in Edward Robinson, *The Original Vision* (Manchester College, Oxford: The Religious Experience Research Unit, 1977), p. 148.

[16] Robert Funk, *Jesus as Precursor* (Philadelphia: Fortress Press, 1975), p. 58.

[17] Cf. Edward Schillebeeckx, *Jesus* (New York: A Crossroad Book, 1979), pp. 256-69.

[18] *Ibid.,* p. 266.

[19] James D.G. Dunn, *Jesus and the Spirit: A Study of the Religious and Charismatic Experience of Jesus and the First Christians as Reflected in the New Testament* (Philadelphia: The Westminster Press, 1975), p. 40.

[20] *Ibid.,* p. 38.

[21] Cf. G.B. Caird, *The Language and Imagery of the Bible* (Philadelphia: The Westminster Press, 1980), Chapter Ten.

[22] *Ibid.,* p. 145.

[23] Robert Hamerton-Kelly, "God the Father in the Bible and in the Experience of Jesus: The State of the Question," *Concilium: God as Father?* (New York: Seabury Press, 1981), p. 101.

[24] Dunn, p. 65.

[25] James Mackey, *Jesus: Man and Myth* (New York: Paulist Press, 1979), pp. 143-44.

[26] Ben Meyer, *The Aims of Jesus* (SCM Press LTD: 1979), p. 161.

[27] Mackey, p. 144.

[28] Ernst Käsemann, *Jesus Means Freedom* (Philadelphia: Fortress Press, 1968).

[29] Mackey, p. 193.

[30] Cf. John F. Haught, *Religion and Self-Acceptance* (New York: Paulist Press, 1976).

[31] William James, "The Divided Self and Conversion," in *Conversion,* ed. Walter E. Conn (New York: Alba House, 1978), p. 128.

[32] *Ibid.*

[33] *Complete Poems of Francis Thompson* (New York: The Modern Library), p. 93.

[34] Cf. Jon Sobrino, *Christology at the Crossroads* (Maryknoll, New York: Orbis Books, 1978).

[35] Norman Perrin, *Rediscovering the Teaching of Jesus* (New York: Harper & Row, 1967), p. 94.

[36] Mackey, pp. 192-93.

[37] Anne Sexton, *The Awful Rowing Toward God* (Boston: Houghton Mifflin Company, 1975), pp. 85-86.

Prayer: The Response of the Contemporary Christian

Doris Donnelly

Only someone living in a hermetically sealed isolation booth could miss the current passion for spirituality. Books on prayer, prayer forms, and models of prayer deluge all of us; retreat centers have been given new leases on life when they respond creatively to the prayer needs of people; courses, programs and conferences on spirituality can usually count on large attendances, and there is an eagerness for the discipline of spiritual growth that few could have predicted in the aftermath of the Second Vatican Council when many traditional religious exercises were jettisoned.

What it all means, I am not sure. I believe, however, that this hunger—and it is frequently described just that way—is more than a fad. For one thing, it is rooted in rich traditions of prayer and scripture and suffers no signs of diminished enthusiasm. Frequently, this prayer is marked by the need for more power to do God's work, by direct experience of the Spirit and by personal love of Jesus. Secondly, this spirituality does not settle for making assembly-line disciples. Quite the contrary. The vigorous rules adopted by Taizé, the Church of the Savior, Koinonia, Sojourners and the Missionary Sisters of Charity, to mention only a few contemporary schools of spirituality, would frighten away all but the most committed brothers and sisters among us. Thirdly, there is evident an increasing sense of the need to connect justice with spirituality. To put it simply, true prayer is filled with compassion for the poor and needy and underprivileged. And something more: that prayer often propels the person who prays—even the

63

timid person who prays—into tumultuous action with a passionate love for righteousness and a willingness to die for the Gospel of Jesus Christ.

True prayer. This is precisely what rests (or ought to rest) at the heart of authentic spirituality for any age. It is only in this kind of prayer that we discover the freedom of listening expectantly to the voice of someone who knows us better than we know ourselves. It is only in this prayer that we begin the journey of a costly, intimate union with a personal God who is at once mystery, master, lover, lord, inconvenience and center of our lives.

The responders to prayer that we will consider know all this better than most. The fact that these responders are all our contemporaries is all to the good, because I believe that, for all the predictability of the spiritual journey—the suffering, the doubt, the consolations, the dark night, the awe, the tears, and the ecstasy—there are new insights, too, and when these are articulated by modern men and women like Teilhard de Chardin, Martin Luther King, Jr., Dorothy Day, Jim Wallis, William Johnston, Evelyn Underhill, Teresa of Calcutta, C.S. Lewis, Dag Hammarskjold and Henri Nouwen, among others, there are freshness, surprise and often an unorthodox quality about them that testify all over again to the inexhaustibility of the Spirit's stirrings wherever it wills.

Dealing with the present, of course, does not exclude the past. In fact, the contemporary Christian's response to prayer, or more particularly to prayer in the 80s, requires that we recognize seeds planted in the 60s and 70s. Contemporary spirituality had a history, and we are now reaping the harvest planted earlier. We are probably planting our own seeds for spirituality in the twenty-first century as well.

Particular accents in spirituality that we are living with came into existence because of movements, pressures, insights, passions and interests that were uncovered and tested by previous generations. If you would allow me to continue my garden metaphor, (and if you saw my vegetable garden last summer, you might think twice about granting this permission), weeds as well as healthy plants have blossomed from these seeds in the first two years of the decade of the 80s. This is a polite way of saying that spirituality now, as in earlier centuries, stands in need of prophets who are strong enough to discern cleverness from wisdom and fakery from transparency because both the chaff and the wheat are, and always have been, present among us.

This *caveat* is particularly important since I have selected four positive and beneficial responses of the contemporary Christian to prayer, or, if the metaphor can be strained, four seeds that fell upon good ground and have yielded much good fruit. These concern the way language, lifestyle, psychology and the East have shaped the responses of our contemporary brothers and sisters.

Language

Since it has direct bearing on all other avenues of discussion, we might just as well begin with the way that many contemporaries have re-interpreted the vocabulary of the geography of the spiritual journey. Paralleling twentieth century insights from sociology and psychology, our contemporary guides avoid the classical *purgative, illuminative* and *unitive* terminology of the past. Instead, they use words like conversion, psychological detachment, discipline and depression rather than purgation; they talk of solitude, paradox and *samadhi*[1] instead of illumination, and of fidelity and intimacy instead of union.

Sometimes it happens that only the language changes, leaving the experience by any other name intact. Most often, however, it is not only a matter of vocabulary; there is a decided different twist in the event as well. Thus, when Dag Hammarskjold, as Secretary General of the United Nations, writes that the palpable presence of Jesus Christ in his life rescued him from brutal loneliness and inevitable suicide, I am quite literally stopped in my tracks and made to take notice because of the proximity of the situation. After all, this is a sophisticated and cultured man of my generation who is speaking; a man who wore three-piece suits, watched TV, rode in taxis, lived in the East Side of Manhattan, presided over an international peace organization and *prayed*—regularly and passionately. If we are to believe his diary, Jesus Christ shifted the emotional equilibrium of his existence and radically changed his life:

> I don't know who—or what—put the question. I don't know when it was put. I don't even remember answering. But at some moment I did answer *yes* to Someone—or Something—and from that hour I was certain that existence is meaningful and that therefore my life in self-surrender had a goal.[2]

Hammarskjold's language and the experiences he describes remind me that prayer language has often been used to camouflage meanings, to keep out whomever it wished, and to separate the big fish from the little pikers. The fact that many of our contemporaries use a vocabulary that people understand and employ a technique they can practice makes prayer accessible to anyone, and opens spirituality, too, so that all may have vision. This is a far cry from a tradition of the early middle ages, reflected in *The Cloud of Unknowing,* which makes an unfortunate distinction between those called to perfection (the contemplatives) and those called to salvation (the actives). For all its difficulty, the contemplative vocation is open to all who would claim it, and Karl Rahner, for one, holds that it is the ordinary development of the grace of baptism.[3] Thomas Merton echoes the sentiment: "Therefore, if anyone should ask, 'Who may desire this gift and pray for it?' the answer is obvious:

Everybody."[4] Quaker Richard Foster agrees: "We must not be led to believe that the Disciplines are for spiritual giants and hence beyond our reach, or for contemplatives who devote all their time to prayer and meditation. Far from it, God intends the Disciplines of the spiritual life to be for ordinary human beings: people who have jobs, who care for children, who must wash dishes and mow lawns."[5]

Furthermore, this more contemporary language for the most part addresses a generation of people in their mid-life or on their second journey. If it is true, as Carl Jung, for one, tells us it is, that there is a receptivity after thirty-five or so for people's spiritual growth and prayer life, then we can rightly acknowledge a *lacuna* in the works of guides of earlier centuries who wrote for teen-age novices in religious communities and stopped there.

Father Gerald O'Collins, S.J., perceptively comments:

> So much 'spirituality' is written for the young, for people still completing their *first* journey. One thinks of Rodriguez (*The Practice of Perfection and Christian Virtues*), and . . . other writers. Rodriguez's volumes came from his conferences for Jesuit novices. Other standard works on the spiritual and religious life were likewise addressed to beginners: the young sister or brother, the seminarian and the newly-ordained priest or minister. The primary audience was intended to be people moving through their late teens on into their late twenties.[6]

All contemporary contemplative persons do not live in religious enclosures, nor does the literature geared at late adolescence or early adult life especially suit them. Thankfully, the works of Evelyn Underhill, Dorothy Sölle and Thomas Merton are powerful enough to capture the imagination and generous idealism of the young, but there is little doubt that they are written mostly for seasoned travelers who have covered enough miles to understand the loneliness, the death of dreams and the painful struggle of starting off at forty or starting over at fifty-five.[7] The wonderful title of Henri Nouwen's book, *The Wounded Healer,* sums it up: It takes time to suffer deep enough wounds and even more time for those wounds to be healed before we can reach out and be of assistance to our brothers and sisters. Wounded healers are more likely to be found at 38 than at 21, and even more come into existence at 50. Contemporary spiritual writers tend to write for that more mature audience.

That audience, incidentally, is what makes up a good part of what we call "church," and it is among that audience of adults that we sense the greatest hunger for guidance in the spiritual life. Christian adults seem to be aware, without too much coaching, that serious prayer life is open to them and no longer belongs exclusively in the cloister. Those same adults may have encouraged the vast numbers of books on spirituality. Or, it could be that the insight of religious writers has paralleled that of secular writers in attending to the mid-life passages of adults.

That passage in mid-life deserves special attention from religious authors because the soil is so ready at that time for spiritual progress. I do not think it accidental to find that *all* of the author/guides I have chosen for this paper come from the mid-life period of the journey themselves.

The frequent concern of these adult travelers is finding guides to be companions in this mid-life spiritual journey. Many adults would say that the church does not have an impressive track-record in providing spiritual guides for all who would seek them. But, that is putting it negatively, and perhaps unfairly. Perhaps I might simply ask two questions:

(1) Are the teachings and experiences of the great schools of spirituality (Benedictine, Franciscan, Dominican, Carmelite, Ignatian) sufficiently accessible to the people of God?

(2) Are *you* a guide for someone undertaking this journey? Think for a moment about this second question. Please do not slither away with, "But I'm a language teacher; it's not my job," or "I used to, but found I didn't have a gift for it." If members of the community cannot turn to you (or me) who have given up today—or maybe this entire week—to learn more about spirituality, to whom can they turn?

And, what are you doing that is more important than being a soul friend to someone else on his or her journey to intimacy with Christ?

Thomas Merton is no longer with us. The ideal *staretz* of desert spirituality is no longer with us. What the church has left is us— sometimes reluctant, unprepared, unexcited us. Moreover, we are what the church *needs* and *wants,* and I greatly support whatever preparation and confidence building are underway to empower persons within a parish, in school and community settings to let this be. I am pleased with Kenneth Leech's choice of the phrase "soul friend" rather than "spiritual director" to describe this relationship.[8] It is far more compatible with the freedom that exists in this context and once again removes the aura of élitism that the vocabulary of "direction" brings with it.

It is not accidental that strides in spiritual intensity are being matched by interest in the kind of companionship that guidance provides. Those who are exploring the world of meditation and silence need the personal guidance that a soul friend gives. The linking of contemplation and action is one of the essential aims of spiritual guidance[9] for the radical Christian, who is steeped in social issues and in danger of losing his or her spiritual roots. For those who have experienced a transforming religious, mystical, or conversion experience, spiritual guidance enables progress so that we are not stunted in our growth in Christ and limited to the most dangerous experience of prayer: begging for an "encore."[10] For any disciple who stands in need of companionship through inner disturbances, spiritual insecurities, joys and new visions, the soul friend is available. Perhaps Kenneth Leech is correct

when he affirms that "never was spiritual direction more urgently
called for than in the present climate of soul searching."[11]

Lifestyle

The call to prayer, and to deep prayer life which is contemplation,
has a hitch to it. The hitch has to do with the love of God and the foolish
things the love of God has us do. In particular, it has to do with the love
of Christ which never remains only the love of Christ but reaches out to
our other brothers and sisters, usually the poor ones, and has a radical
effect on our lifestyle.

"Being in love with God . . . is being in love in an unrestricted
fashion,"[12] wrote Bernard Lonergan. He continues: "All love is self-
surrender, but being in love with God is being in love without limits or
qualifications or conditions or reservations."[13] This kind of love has
explosive and unexpected consequences, and prime among them is the
fact that it is incarnational in that it is not love of God divorced from
love of the world. Nor is it love of God that encourages us to deny, or
even worse, to hate the world. Rather, it is a love that enables us to find
the spatial, material world vibrating with the presence of Christ.

Surely a splendid guide in this area is Pierre Teilhard de Chardin
who talked of "spiritualized matter," and who understood the incarnation of Jesus Christ into our human world as a landmark in the evolu-
tionary process. Since the coming of Christ, according to Teilhard, we
have been propelled into Christogenesis, a sphere characterized by the
presence of the cosmic Christ who is vitally engaged in the material
universe and who is drawing that universe by the power of love to its
fullness and completion.[14]

There is little doubt in my mind that the best way to understand
Teilhard de Chardin is through his poetic and practical book, *The
Divine Milieu.* Significantly, it is dedicated to "those who love the
world," and Teilhard was aware, probably more keenly than the rest of
us, of the pervasive sense among Christians that the more they separated themselves from the world, the nearer they would come to God.
As an antidote, Teilhard offered a way of thinking that showed how *all
our actions,* secular as well as religious, can be divinized, or consecrated,
and allow us to "put on Christ" and live in an intimate union with
him. As if that were not enough, Teilhard then explained, with fresh
vocabulary and insight, how every work of ours possessed intrinsic
value because it was part of God's great reintegration of all things in
Christ (Ephesians 1:10). Teilhard writes:

> He awaits us every instant in our action, in the work of the moment.
> There is a sense in which he is at the tip of my pen, my spade, my brush,
> my needle—of my heart and of my thought.[15]

I wonder whether it helps to be a paleontologist, working in the earth, to understand all of this. Or a contemplative—because their insights are so similar. Both would hold that prayer, the core of all religious experience, has led to the most dynamic and revolutionary action. I believe that those who pray are enlightened by virtue of their identity with Christ to stretch out from that vertical relationship into the horizontal one and to love those whom He loves.

Prayer at this level even allows us to be one with the person we love. Surely that is true of our relationship with Christ, but the point is that because of that loving relationship, we share the mission of Teilhard's cosmic Christ and reach out with Christ's hands to the needs of the wider family. It is even possible through the love of Christ to empathize at such a profound level that we become part of others to such an extent that what happens to them happens to us.

There was a time in the history of Christian spirituality when one could make a decision about becoming a contemplative *or* an active follower. It is no longer an either-or decision; there is no longer a separation of the haves and the have nots.[16]

It is very simply a matter now of deciding what form your contemplation-in-action is going to take. The fact that rigorous, disciplined prayer life leads to solidarity with our brothers and sisters is axiomatic. How that solidarity works itself out is open to a variety of approaches from deciding, like Mother Teresa, to live out one's life picking up the destitute from the streets of Calcutta or spending one's days in a cave or a monastery as did Thomas Merton.

Merton is especially helpful because he has left testimony, in language that we can understand, that his prayer life in a monastery connected him, inexplicably, with the sufferings of humankind. An Anglican friend, Mark Gibbard, wrote in this connection of Merton:

> Thomas Merton advocated nuclear pacifism in the coldest days of the cold war. He pleaded for disengagement from Vietnam long before American students were marching and protesting. He sensed the coming to Black Power, and already in 1963 he wrote *Letters to a White Liberal* to wake others up. He was in touch with avant-garde poets in South America, corresponding with them in Portuguese and Spanish.[17]

Merton himself sensed his corporateness in the Body of Christ in a most unforgettable and mysterious way on his way to a dentist appointment in Louisville, outside the Gethsemani enclosure. Merton wrote:

> In Louisville, at the corner of Fourth Avenue and Walnut Street, in the center of the shopping district, I was suddenly overwhelmed with the realization that I loved all these people, that they were mine and I theirs . . . It was like waking from a dream of separateness . . . This sense of liberation from an illusory difference was such a relief and joy to me that I almost laughed out loud . . . To think that such a commonplace

realization should suddenly seem like news that one holds the winning ticket in a cosmic sweepstake.[18]

I introduced Merton's witnessing by claiming this happened in a mysterious way. Maybe it is not so mysterious, after all. If we have ever had a glimpse of the effect of prayer (in someone else's life or our own) as the place where we confront our own dependencies, insecurities, helplessness, loneliness, and sinfulness, we know we can learn a great deal about nature—human and divine—in prayer. We likewise are able to identify with the triumphs, struggles, needs and joys of the human heart because we have met all these things inside ourselves as well. Thus, it should not surprise us in the least to find Henri Nouwen writing from the Trappist Abbey at Genesee, New York, that it was there (and not at Yale Divinity School where he was teaching at the time, or on a lecture tour in Asia) that he keenly felt the weight of the war in Vietnam and the agony of Watergate.[19]

Similarly, Teilhard de Chardin, travelling across the Gobi desert for days on end, could write:

> Since once again, Lord—though this time not in the forests of the Aisne but in the steppes of Asia—I have neither bread, nor wine, nor altar . . . I, your priest, will make the whole earth my altar and on it will offer you all the labours and sufferings of the world . . . One by one, Lord, I see and I love all those whom you have given me to sustain and charm my life . . . I call before me the whole vast anonymous army of living humanity.[20]

The point is that we must never underestimate the wisdom of the desert. For the fact is that "the person who has spent long periods in authentic prayer and meditation knows about the suffering of the world because he (she) has experienced it all within himself (herself)."[21]

I do not know any more of "how" this happens, but I do know without any doubt that prayer and solidarity are inseparably linked. "We are not to love just platonically and keep it all inside us," wrote René Voillaume, "we are to live with a love that comforts and succours, with a love that helps to bear pain, with a love that spreads joy."[22]

Thomas Merton linked the solitude dimension of prayer to solidarity. Commenting on this connection in Merton, Kenneth Leech observed that "it is in solitude that one attains a deepening of awareness of the world's needs. In solitude, too, one attains an identification with the sufferings of Christ in the world."[23] I, too, believe that this is so. I also do not find it difficult to believe that this can happen—that it *does* happen—in a hermitage in a Trappist Abbey. Prayer, true prayer, transcends those barriers lithely. John Eudes Bamberger, O.C.S.O., currently Abbot of Genesee, but once fellow-monk with Tom Merton at Gethsemani, confirms these speculations when he wrote of Merton:

> We came to see that when he spoke with compassion for the oppressed of the earth, he spoke out of an awareness bought with his own anguish of heart and won by contemplative effort and insight. We saw that he was compassionate because he knew himself as having received the compassion of God.[24]

I have dwelt lengthily on this subject of contemplation-in-action because it endures such indifference among Christians. There are those who would hold that some of us should identify with the poor while others might ignore that aspect of discipleship. To these, I would simply reaffirm that prayer that does not reach out to embrace others may be many things, even many good things, but it is not prayer. I have gone out of my way to muster up evidence from Thomas Merton, sequestered as he was in a remote monastery, as corroboration that *no one* is excused from this extension of prayer.

But, there is more, and the more has to do with the concrete ways that prayer touches the lives of the rest of us who live with two feet "in the world." Not the least among a very impressive line-up of role models who have gone ahead of us in this regard is Dorothy Day.

The title of William Miller's biography of Dorothy Day, *A Harsh and Dreadful Love,* derived from *The Brothers Karamazov,* epitomizes the radical motivation of Dorothy Day and the Catholic Worker movement. Concerning this "active love" that so motivated Dorothy Day, Father Zossima, the monk in the novel, explains in words what Dorothy Day has many times repeated:

> Love in action is a harsh and dreadful thing compared to love in dreams. Love in dreams is greedy for immediate action, rapidly performed and in the sight of all . . . But active love is labour and fortitude . . . When you see with horror that in spite of all your efforts you are getting further from your goal instead of nearer to it—at that very moment you will reach and behold clearly the miraculous power of the Lord who has been all the time loving and mysteriously guiding you.[25]

The need to put this "active love" into practice led Dorothy Day and her cohort Peter Maurin to the publication of *The Catholic Worker* as the vehicle by which their mutual concern "for the poor and the oppressed" could be publicized. It is hard to say how much Dorothy Day influenced the institutional church, in life or in death. There was influence, to be sure, but at best it nicked at and permeated the edges of a church which attempts to be a church of the poor without being a poor church.

Dorothy Day lived the poor church.

A newspaper editoral, written when Day died in 1980, said this:

She did not say hers was the only way. She did not vote. She did not pay taxes. But these were the small things. She *did* offer up her life for the least. She *did* oppose war—pacifically and nonviolently. She did not yield. Which is not to suggest she ever saw herself as anything other than ordinary. But she was an ordinary *Christian*. And that tells us all how far we have yet to go.[26]

Without for a minute denying her uniqueness, one realizes it is also true that there are always new Dorothys—or new Oscar Romeros, or Steven Bikos, or Martin Luther King, Jrs.—in this and in other countries, with messages of liberation and oneness with the oppressed.

— There is among us now the voice of the German theologian, Dorothy Sölle, to remind us in one of the poems from her collection, *Revolutionary Patience:*

> He needs you
> that's all there is to it
> without you he's left hanging
> goes up in dachau's smoke
> is sugar and spice in the baker's hands
> gets revalued in the next stock market crash
> he's consumed and blown away
> used up
> without you
>
> Help him
> that's what faith is
> he can't bring it about
> his kingdom
> couldn't then couldn't later can't now
> not at any rate without you
> and that is his irresistible appeal[27]

— There is the voice of Segundo Galilea who maintains, quite simply, that "in Catholic spirituality, this sense of the poor appears as inseparable from the meaning of God, so that a conversion to the Lord always implies as an important dimension, a turning to the poor."[28]

— There is the voice of Archbishop Raymond J. Hunthausen who claims that the more he prayed and the more he read, the more he understood the need to be leader and shepherd among his people, especially on nuclear disarmament.[29]

— There is the voice of Jim Wallis and the Sojourners community who, thankfully, are keeping before us the issues of injustice and our national culpability in Latin America. If Dorothy Day lived the poor church, the Sojourners live the suffering and persecuted church.

These are some of the voices talking to us, as Dorothy did. The question is, *are we listening?* I suspect that the issues of lifestyle and contemplation-in-action will nag at us until we make peace with them, each in his/her own way.

Psychology

During the 1960s and early 70s—the time of the seed plantings for the spirituality of the 80s—I lived in California where I met Dorothy Day, as well as Cesar Chavez and Roy Wilkins, each for the first time. During those years, the West Coast was the mecca for every new movement under and about the sun. It was *the* place to be, and it was an overwhelming experience for a very formal Easterner who owned neither sandals nor a pair of cut-off jeans. I was a Democratic campaign worker in Los Angeles on the day Robert Kennedy was assassinated there; I watched the burning of Watts from the Palos Verdes Hills; and I lived for a time in a house less than a half mile from where Charles Manson and his "family" went on one of their bloody escapades.

As a twenty-one-year-old New Yorker transplanted to Los Angeles, I was continuously exposed to protest and racial riots that seethed in the atmosphere I breathed. I lived and loved and taught there for ten years, sometimes as if I were an alien on a strange planet. My students talked of vibes (theirs and mine), karma (theirs and mine), free love (theirs), and where to get the best grass (theirs). For several years, my teaching took place at Immaculate Heart College, famous for its extraordinary faith commitment in a bewildered culture as well as for its splendid serigraphs by Sister Corita. I remember that I was having lunch in the IHM dining room on the late fall day that Sister Corita wrote to Sister Anita Caspary of her intention to leave the Community. Another illusion of permanence was shattered. That, as I remember it, is what the 60s were about: dreams collapsing, and new and painful substitutes taking their place.

If I were to tell you of the over-riding pre-occupation that I associate with California in the 1960s, it would not be LSD trips, Esalen, surfing or films like "Easy Rider" and "The Graduate." Rather, it would be the avidity with which the world of psychology was consumed. To me, there is no question that the popularization of psychology left its imprint on prayer, and that we are seeing the ramifications of that influence now.

Psychology helped us probe our conscious and unconscious minds and opened up an understanding of prayer that let us speak about how God penetrated all levels of consciousness and even our dream world. I still write occasional entries in my dream diary, and I have been helped in knowing how God is speaking to me as I unravel their not-so-enigmatic-after-all meanings. There was a time when over half my students in a class I was conducting in spiritual theology (in New York

City, not in L.A.) were attending to their dreams, sometimes with astonishing consequences.

It is now over ten years since that class first met, yet I remember, without any difficulty, the first dream presented by one of the students.

A good-looking twenty-one-year-old senior remembered that in his dream he was driving alone as a passenger in the rear seat of a car. In the front seat were his parents and an older brother. The student noticed that the car was passing his destination, but that no one stopped for him to get out. He was temporarily paralyzed and did not know how to get out either. The dreamer awoke in a state of panic.

One of the reasons that I recall this dream with such clarity is that *fully one quarter* of the class related similar dreams. A young woman dreamed that she was flying an airplane alone on a gorgeous day, doing stunts and acrobatics. A throng of admirers gathered in a field below. Suddenly, the woman realized she did not know how to land the plane, and she woke up in a cold sweat. A graduate student told of a dream in which he took a school bus on a joy ride until it ran out of gas and he was forced to walk—to someplace. He could not see any destination before him because of a heavy fog.

All of these dreams tell different stories, but the common denominators were more startling than the differences.[30] Among those common denominators, the dreams indicated some anxiety about the futures that these students faced; they told of how passive many felt the educational process was and how hesitant or panicked they were about pursuing the next steps in their lives. One student recognized how often he took the "back seat" in the decision making process and how infrequently he used his own talent and will and effort in working out his own destiny and personal development.

For all the students in this group, it was curious how the dreams did not tell them what to do; they merely pictured situations *as the unconscious viewed them,* leaving it up to the dreamers in their consciousness to take action or not, *as they chose.*

We also noted how helpful students were to each other in interpreting dreams (or parts of dreams) that stumped the dreamer. Frequently enough, another person who had lived through a similar experience could help unravel a hitherto mysterious part of a dream.

Psychology also reminded us that having emotions was normal and healthy. It taught us how to differentiate between growth and destructive emotions and helped us to cultivate one and handle the other. I attended and conducted enough retreats and days of prayer in the 60s (and since) to know hundreds of liberating occasions when someone understood again or for the first time that emotions in prayer were O.K. and that prayer was not the place where we had to stifle who we were so as not to displease God who wanted things ship-shape before talking to us. I recall that in 1974, when the film *Network* was released with its recurrent refrain, "I'm so damned mad, and I'm not going to take it any more," I could reminisce (not all too happily) of the many times in the 60s when I heard those words addressed to God, usually signaling the end of a relationship. Emotions. God knows, we are indebted to the 60s for "getting in touch with them" and "sharing them" to the point of nausea. We are also indebted for clarity and guidance in this area that facilitated growth and freedom for many.

It was also possible, thanks to the popularization of psychology, to analyze and to reconstruct our negative behavior. I saw how the patient, nonthreatening, nonjudgmental love of a therapist helped in a transformation process that frequently was nothing short of a miracle. I learned a great many healing techniques from the therapeutic world, not the least of which was how to listen to another so that the gradual process of self-revelation and self-discovery could occur.

I trust that you hear in my words a profound respect for the world of psychology, so that I can relate another side to it all that was also present, though in a lighter vein. The truth is that often enough, no human experience was too insignificant to escape notice—each idiosyncracy, each aberration was entitled to close scrutiny—and the adventure of analyzing them was not for the fainthearted. Marathon sessions were called to get to the bottom of things, and I remember learning from one of these thirty-six hour episodes that my sanity would be at stake if I ever participated in another one. I never have.

Yet, I learned from all of this to be more reflective of my human experience, to be less rigid and more open, or in the vernacular of the time, "to hang loose." This was worth whatever dues I had to pay. This lesson, more than any other, has greatly influenced how I do adult religious education because I have come to see that, for an adult, it is not experience that matters, but rather it is reflection on experience that is the key to transformation.

The fact of the matter is, to cite an example, the disciples on the road to Emmaus (Luke 24) had many experiences. Any number of these took place with one of the most significant religious leaders the world has ever known, yet the experiences did not seem to amount to a hill of beans. They walked next to Jesus, and they did not even recognize him!

A myth exists that we learn from our experiences, and it is just that: a myth. The truth is that we learn nothing from raw experiences, but we learn everything from reflecting on our experiences by probing and coaxing them and making connections so that the "Aha!" of recognition can take place. It was only when the Emmaus disciples reflected on their experiences: "Did not our hearts burn within us?" (v. 32), that something important happened. They moved from knowing about Jesus to experiencing Jesus. What a difference!

Something similar happened in the story of the beggar Lazarus and the Rich Man (Luke 16). Diseased and covered with sores during his lifetime, Lazarus was comforted after his death "and was carried by the angels to Abraham's bosom" (v. 22). "Suffering the torments of Hades, the Rich Man begged Abraham to send Lazarus to his five brothers so that he may warn them, lest they also come into this place of torment" (v. 28). The Rich Man knew his brothers well. He knew they were accumulating many experiences (as he did), but that they needed (as he did) to reflect on them. He felt sure that if they reflected and confronted themselves, they would change.

The current interest in psychology, with its techniques for journal keeping and dream analysis, provides wonderful aids for the reflection process.

Given this concentration, I wonder whether it surprises you as much as it does me to find such poor reception among Roman Catholics for the sacrament of penance—the supreme enabler of the reflective and transforming process. It is curious that with business booming for the psychologist, the same cannot be said for the "business" of the confessor. I think it would serve us well to observe this phenomenon a bit more closely.

First of all, the 1974 revised *Rite of Penance*[31] takes three forms. The first of these involves individual confession and reconciliation of penitents; the second form involves individual confession in a corporate community setting; the third involves general confession and general absolution. The *Praenotanda* of the *Rite of Penance* advise that Rite C be used only with approval of the ordinary or with report to him afterwards of the circumstances of its use. Suffice it to say that, in general, Rite C is not used with any regularity in the United States. This practice may well change with the upcoming Synod of Bishops in 1983, but for now this is the case. That leaves Rites A and B. Of these, admittedly Rite A is infrequently used. It is frequently equated with the older way of "going to confession" each week in long Saturday night lines, and it always and everywhere falls short in comparison when head counts take place.

There is, however, good news in all of this. The good news takes place in conjunction with Rite B. When it is carefully planned for (proper catechesis, informed preaching, prayerful atmosphere, appropriate music and sufficient numbers of confessors), huge numbers of prayerful penitents participate in the sacrament. A former student of mine nonchalantly told me that at the church he pastors in Brooklyn more than a thousand persons participate in form B of the sacrament of penance at a communal service each of two times that it is celebrated in the course of a year.

I read all of this as a very hopeful sign. The privatized, anonymous practice of the sacrament in the past simply will no longer do as an experience for contemporary Catholics. Instead, there is insistence on an understanding of personal as well as collective sin within a communal setting that is being affirmed and vigorously celebrated in Rite B. Appreciation for Rite B is justified insofar as:

— Rite B respects both personal sin and its effects within the community. In the context of this ritual, it is impossible to imagine sin as an individual act of disobedience that has no ramifications within the community at large.
— Rite B affirms our corporate involvement in systemic social sins like violence, racism and sexism and claims that while we are part of the problem, through repentance and God's holiness we are also part of the solution.
— Rite B claims that all of us are in need of repentance: the old and the young, the rich and the poor, men and women, all societies, classes and *even the church* itself. No one belongs to an exclusive sinless club.

One other fact needs mentioning, and it concerns how appreciative some Protestants have been for insights dimmed or forgotten by Roman Catholics on the subject of reconciliation.

Baptist minister John Claypool strongly encouraged his congregation to renew their appreciation for a rite and ritual to surround the experience of acknowledging our sins to another Christian. "Protestants talked a great deal about the forgiveness of God," Claypool once preached, "but we forgot how *to do* confession and repentance and the receiving of forgiveness. As a result, for many . . . we do not know how to get rid of our sins. We continue to carry around the whole load of the past without any relief."[32]

The power of confession was brought home to me most recently by the Quaker Richard Foster. Foster recalls that he did not take the step of confessing to another out of any deep burden of sin. It was prompted, instead, by a longing for more power to do the work of God. "I felt inadequate for many of the desperate needs with which I was confronted," he writes.[33]

While reviewing his life, Foster remained assured that God would reveal anything that needed healing. He then went "to a dear brother in Christ" and read from a sheet of paper on which he listed his sins, adding only those comments necessary to make the sin clear.

> When I had finished, I began to return the paper to my briefcase. Wisely, my counselor-confessor gently stopped my hand and took the sheet of paper. Without a word he took a wastebasket, and as I watched he tore the paper into hundreds of tiny pieces and dropped them into the basket. That powerful nonverbal expression of forgiveness was followed by a simple absolution. My sins I knew were as far away as the East is from the West.
>
> Next my friend, with the laying on of hands, prayed a prayer of healing for all of the sorrows and hurts of the past. The power of that prayer lives with me today.
>
> There was one interesting sidelight. The exposure of my humanity evidently sparked a freedom in my counselor-friend, for directly

following his prayer for me he was able to express a deep and troubling sin that he had been unable to confess until then. Freedom begets freedom.[34]

If freedom and power are gifts of the sacrament of penance in the Roman Catholic tradition, those insights, articulated by Richard Foster, have been blurred in its practice. It is curious to observe how much energy and excitement can be derived from a ritual we simply took for granted.

The good news, of course, is that because of the vision of people apart from a Roman Catholic background and because of the wisdom of the field of psychology, we are able to take a new look at some old truths concerning the archetypical need to confess one's sins and to be pardoned. There are few things more effective than having the one looking in on us tell us the value of what we are missing.

In a nutshell, I think that is what psychology has done for us: it has reaffirmed the importance of internal as well as external freedom that has always rested at the heart of prayer. In so doing, it has offered some valuable keys to the transformation process that stand us in good stead in our efforts in pastoral ministry, counseling, penance and prayer.

The East

Lastly, there is the matter of our learning from the East. I have saved this for the end, partially because it is foreign in language, thought and style; partially because it is subject to the most misunderstanding; and partially because I yielded to some inner impulse to keep these remarks separated from other comments derived from the background of Western spirituality.

A great many people know a lot more about this subject area than I do, and many are more faithful to its disciplines than I. And, while I blithely remind you of how foreign all of it is, I am sure you are aware of its astonishing popularity here in America. So many of those who desire to meditate have learned from those versed in Eastern ways of meditation both a rationale and a practice. We have schools of yoga, zen and transcendental meditation listed in many city telephone directories, and Morton Kelsey, for one, suggests that "it would be hard to guess how many students (and professors) have felt an impelling need to try out these methods."[35] The suggestion even comes from Herbert Benson at Harvard that the business community replace their coffee break with a demystified form of TM. He proposes this practice as a specific way of making employees happier and increasing the level of profit.[36]

For all of this, I am strangely drawn to the wisdom, style, discipline and teaching of the Orient and to what non-Christian religious traditions continue to teach me about prayer. As a disciple, I happen to be in very good company, and I have found the insights of Thomas Merton[37] and William Johnston[38] to be of inestimable value on this part of my journey.

On this matter of journey, it is only fair to admit that my interest does not stem from any trip I took to the Orient. In fact, I have never visited Japan, but long to do so, not especially as a tourist but as a seeker who might sit at the feet of a *roshi* and learn.[39] The truth of the matter is that I have saved this topic for last probably because there is a kinship with it that will not go away, and in many ways, it is closest of all to my heart.

I frequently hesitate to talk about the East as a special interest of mine because it is so frequently misunderstood as "wacky" and "far out." I do not especially enjoy the strange caricatures this evokes in people, and my vanity (as well as the truth) resists being pictured as wrapped in saffron robes, following strangers at airports, pinning flowers on your lapels or dresses, sitting lotus-style in my dining room, feeding my guests dewdrops and geranium seeds for supper. I recall once, after lecturing on what Christian meditation could learn from Zen, a gentleman approached me at the end of my talk. "I hope you think it over before you let them shave your head," he advised as he wagged a finger at me. An hour later, I saw him again on the cafeteria line. "See that girl," he commanded in boisterous tones to another diner. "She's giving up the Catholic Church to become a swami."

The paradox is that my faith in the Catholic Church and my prayer life have been strengthened and expanded because of my exposure to the East. It has done so through insights on detachment, imageless prayer, the body and silence that I have (at least in part) made my own.

The Zen teaching on detachment has been of great assistance to me.[40] Basically, it holds that clinging is the great obstacle to prayer, and that clinging takes a variety of shapes and forms. The most obvious attachments have to do with material things, with possessions and with desires of the human heart, like success and achievement that are difficult to surrender because every inch of the way they require a death to self. Then, there is the clinging to our anxieties, those things one would think we would most like to be rid of, but which seduce us simply because they are so familiar and because, after a while, they have become part of us. As a result, we actually cling to our anxieties, scrupulosities, guilt, nostalgia, and fears about the future. The Buddhist says, "Let go." Jesus says, "Do not be anxious about your life" (Mtt. 6:25). "Do not be afraid."

In this area of detachment, Zen is all very compatible with Christian teaching, but once again, I think the new vocabulary on the subject enabled me to take a fresh look at what was being said. And, what was being said is that the Gospel teaching that we renounce mother and father and sister and brother means just that. It means that in order to follow Jesus and to claim him as our only security, we must not cling to anyone or anything but him; we must not hedge our bets by clinging to

other things in addition to him (just in case religion and Jesus fail us).
We must not even cling to good things: our families, our gifts, our
vocations; we must be willing to surrender everything. Non-clinging
means, quite precisely, non-clinging.

Perhaps, a short illustration here will clarify all these words. I have
taken special interest in how the world press reports Mother Teresa's
involvement with the poor. She is pictured as serving them, loving
them, saving them, healing them and sometimes, as even *living for them*.
This last statement is a most distressing characterization because it is
incorrect. Because Mother Teresa is genuine and, it would seem to
many of us, holy, it is enlightening to hear how she herself talks of her
service to the poor:

> During the mass, I said (to the sisters), "you saw that the priest touched
> the body of Christ with great love and tenderness. *When you touch the poor
> today, you will be touching the body of Christ.* Give them that same love and
> tenderness." When they returned several hours later, the new sister
> came up to me, her face shining with joy. "I have been touching the
> body of Christ for three hours," she said. I asked her what she had done.
> "Just as we arrived, the sister brought in a man covered with maggots.
> He had been picked up from a drain. I have been taking care of him, I
> have been touching Christ. I knew it was him," she said.[41]

This is a most amazing statement.

The point is that Mother Teresa does not cling to the poor; she clings
to Christ . . . even when she is *serving* the poor. This happens because
she is able to identify Christ with the poor—no mean feat, mind you—
so that when she gives the cup of water to the leper, Mother Teresa
would remain unconvinced by you or by me that it was a leper and not
Christ himself. Mother Teresa possesses enough freedom to know that
even to be attached to the poor, or to cling to them, would be as serious
an idolatry as clinging to anything else and would stand in the way of
her unity with Christ. Mother Teresa is right on target. She knows
what many of us are still struggling to integrate into our own lives: the
wisdom of letting go.

Actually, Zen pushes this detachment business one step further and
suggests the need to be detached not only from persons and things and
anxieties, but also from thinking itself. It is possible, Zen explains, not
only to live in the world of ideas but to cling to these ideas as well. Worst
of all, it is possible to cling to ideas and thoughts and words *about God* so
that our prayer lives remain perpetually discursive and chatty and
forever miss the splendor and intimacy that come to the one who
contemplates. There is a world of difference between prayer (between
any relationship, for that matter) that is born of curiosity, always
asking questions, always meditating "on something," and prayer that
is born of wonder which simply beholds the Other and connects on
some deep level of speechless oneness. Zen is all for this speechless

oneness, and Zen meditation is filled with suggestions that assist Christian prayer to be at that level. There are many of these suggestions, adapted from Zen, so permit me to limit myself to three:

(1) Zen tells us that when thoughts and ideas go and we enter the void, we need help to focus our energies and our selves to discover the hidden self. Do not be put off by this manner of speaking. Zen is alerting the Christian to the need for focusing once we put down the New Testament or the devotional book we are reading. Otherwise, we are distracted unnecessarily by class notes and shopping lists and letters that need to be written. That focusing is helped by a word that rhythmically centers us on the presence of Christ within us: "Healer." "Brother." "Savior." Or, it is helped by a steady gaze, eyes half-closed, on the sanctuary lamp near the tabernacle, or by a crucifix not there for us to think about but for us to be with in our journey to the center of our beings where Christ is present but dormant because we do not know how to free him or ourselves.

Clutter in prayer, just like clutter in our other relationships, distracts us from "who" is there. Much of the clutter and busy-ness of our prayer lives (and I leave it for all of us to assess how true this is in your other relationships) has to do with verbosity, with words, words, words that distract us from going deeper, deeper, deeper. All of this is compounded for us Westerners by the way we have been taught to pray: we are encouraged to read scripture and to mull over the events of Jesus' life and to talk with Jesus before establishing applicability of the whole enterprise to our lives. Few of us have been taught prayer that is not dependent on thinking; fewer still know how to rid our prayer of thoughts that we cling to for want of anything else "to do."

The dilemma we face is amusingly depicted by Jesuit William Johnston in his charming book, *Silent Music*. Father Johnston had the opportunity to visit with Dr. Joseph Kamiya of the Langley Porter Institute in San Francisco and to hear about bio-feedback testing that had been done to register alpha levels of various gurus and roshi. Alpha rhythm is associated with more advanced meditation and mysticism. As it happened, many of those Zen and Buddhist meditators quickly and facilely registered high-amplitude alpha waves which indicated that the subjects were in a rather deep state of concentration. In a flash of inspiration, Father Johnston asked why the staff at Langley Porter did not test some Christian monks. "They replied that they did. They tested some Catholic clergymen. But whereas the yogis and masters sat silently in majestic splendour registering exquisite and impeccable alpha, the (Catholic) clergymen read the Bible, sang hymns, wandered around the room and fouled up the machines."[42]

(2) The Oriental religions remind the Christian how important the body is for contemplation and meditation. This is not quite true. What Oriental religions do is remind the Christian that *integrating* body and spirit is important for prayer. Too often Westerners have held on to the

pathetic dichotomy that suggests that we pray with our hearts and that if our bodies balk at the effort, it is a small price to pay. If truth be told, I think there was some unwritten law that suggested that our heart prayers were probably more efficacious if the body was in pain.

Zen shows us what it looks like to pray with the whole person and how meditation is an art that teaches the use of eyes, lungs, abdomen, spine and all the rest. He or she says that the lotus posture is not only aesthetically pleasing but physiologically helpful because it induces a straight back which, in turn, induces rhythmic and slow abdominal breathing which, in turn, slows down the heartbeat, all of which is conducive to prayer. It is only in this context that the Jesus Prayer makes sense. The Jesus Prayer is a way of inviting the presence of Christ into our being by slowly repeating the words, "Jesus, Son of David, have mercy on me." Some recommend that we breathe in on the first half of the prayer, and out on the second half.

The point is that it is most unlikely to engage in the Jesus Prayer if we are hyperventilating, breathing erratically or huffing and puffing. Zen counsels regarding prayer are wonderful first steps in moving from cerebral to more affective and visceral prayer.

I do not know whether I would be as sold as I am on this subject of breathing and integrating the body in prayer if it were not for an operation I underwent at the time of my son's birth almost fourteen years ago. After Caesarean surgery, a helpful and informed nurse explained how much I could do to relieve abdominal pain by breathing exercises that would relax muscles and lessen tension during my hospital stay. Whenever I put her advice into practice, I realized how stiffly my body lay in bed. As soon as I followed her advice, I experienced a wonderful release both of pressure and pain. It was a great help.

Many of my women friends have confirmed to me that the same theory lies behind Lamaze natural childbirth instruction: Have your body (especially your breathing) work with you and not against you. The husband of one of these friends applied the breathing technique to his migraine headaches with some success.

We have incorporated this principle into the activities of our little family. We are hardly Stoics: we take our novocain at the dentist like the rest of the human race. But, if you listen closely, you will hear the advice of one Donnelly to another: "Breathe slowly and evenly." And, each of us knows it works.

We are, however, talking about breathing and prayer, and the connections are similarly effective. I do not know a better way of entering the prayer experience than through the quieting process that happens in controlled breathing. At first, I was very self-conscious about my efforts in this regard. Not only did the process of waiting for the indwelling of Christ (at the point when the Jesus prayer "takes over" and I no longer "recite" it) seem to be excessively time-consuming, but it also appeared contrived and gimmicky. If you share any of these fears or concerns, perhaps I can allay them by testifying to the gentle surrender that breathing evokes in me. As hurried and harried as I have been before prayer, the simple formula of breathing in the presence of Jesus Christ with the Jesus Prayer or a word like "Redeemer," and breathing out my cares, concerns, and all that is distracting to this relationship while I exhale, has a marvelous way of centering me. There may be better ways or more sophisticated ways; that I do not dispute. What I know is that for me this key unlocks the door to contemplation with the least amount of fuss and effort.

(3) My last comments have to do with the experience of solitude that is also mediated to us by the East.

I would be among the first to concede that there was often a rapture that surrounded the hushed adoration of the Blessed Sacrament at "Benediction" or "Forty Hours" when I was growing up in the Church. Those quiet moments have been displaced in recent years by guitars, four-piece combos, lengthier sermons and more vocal prayers. A liturgy council at a local parish recently advised their pastor that there was a need for some quiet prayer time during the Sunday Eucharist. The pastor agreed and implemented a plan for two minutes of silence *after* (not during) the last collection. Fidgeting began after thirty seconds; nudging after one minute. Finally, a woman seated closest to the sanctuary left her pew to get a closer look at the pastor, presumably to determine whether he was still alive. A good section of the congregation thought he forgot what "to do" next. Heaven forbid that there be worshipful silence in our churches!

Yet, you would need only to scratch any theology of prayer and the spiritual life for its blueprint of maturity or holiness, to be counseled to seek solitude. One eminent guide, Teresa of Avila, suggested: "Settle yourself in solitude and you will come upon Him in yourself." The solitude in question is of the inner variety—a solitude of heart that can be maintained in the midst of noise because its roots are deep and unflappable. External silence is usually a means to that peaceful and serene kind of solitude, but silence, as we all know, is never a guarantee of solitude. In the literature of the hesychast tradition, the Eastern Christian tradition you may recognize at the heart of *The Way of a Pilgrim,* Abba Poemen advised:

> One (person) appears to be keeping silent and yet condemns others in his/her heart: such a person is speaking all the time. Another (person) talks from morning till evening and yet keeps silent; that is, he/she says nothing except what is helpful to others. [43]

This solitude of the heart is precisely what is needed by contemporary men and women in their response to prayer. It is a lesson that Eastern Christianity as well as Eastern Oriental religions like Zen and Zen Buddhism never lost sight of. I learned from these Eastern guides as well as their counterparts in the West what the benefits of solitude are. Most of my guides would agree that those benefits come quickly and that there are at least three of them.

(A) *Solitude Puts Us in Contact with Reality.* An old proverb puts it succinctly: "People who open their mouths, close their eyes." That is another way of saying that the purpose of solitude is to enable us to see and hear.

It is, mercifully, not our own reflection that we see, nor is it our own voice that we hear because we have yielded control of our tongues to vindicate and justify and manipulate. One of the fruits of silence is that we let our justification rest entirely with God. We surrender our need to set the story straight. We resist the urge to prove how right we are, how misjudged we were, how unfairly we were treated.

We are all familiar with the counsel, "Sleep on it," when an important decision has to be made and we feel we may not be directed by our best interest. Solitude provides the occasion to do something similar to sleeping: a slowing down takes place, a quieting of the inside and outside, a sensing of the greatness of the world about us, and a greater awareness of some serious and major concerns become real to us. "We have to slow down the movement on the outside," Dag Hammarskjold said, "to pay attention to the voices within."[44] In our own lives, we become conscious of our own resources and those of our faith. In quiet, we face our fears and our worries with a realistic assessment that there are powers at work other than our own.

In *Celebration of Discipline,*[45] Richard J. Foster suggests that we find or develop a "quiet place" designed for silence and solitude. Consider incorporating into the plans for a new house an inner sanctuary, a small place where any family member could go to be alone and silent. Why not? We build elaborate game rooms, TV rooms, family rooms and play rooms and think they are well worth the expense. If you already own a home or live in an apartment, you might designate part of a room or even a chair as special. Whenever anyone is in it, he or she is saying, "Please don't bother me, I want to be alone."

(B) *Solitude Helps Us Become Centered.* The centering experience is the heart of solitude and is probably best explained by its opposite. The underside of centering is a sense of fragmentation: hundreds of responsibilities, projects and concerns freefloating without a core. Anne Morrow Lindbergh, a helpful guide in matters of solitude since her famous retreat to the Maine Coast while she was the mother of five young children and the wife of one of our country's greatest celebrities, refers to the German word *zerreisenheit* to describe this feeling.[46] "Torn-to-piece hood," it is translated, and we all know the feeling that Lindbergh is talking about. Not only are the spokes flying wild when *zerreisenheit* is being felt, but it is also accompanied by a fear that the pieces will never be put back together again.

Centering counteracts that fear. Centering allows us to rearrange our lives and to focus at the heart of all that we are about, a power base that energizes our activities. It inspires a "collectedness" which is the sphere we must enter if we really want to get hold of ourselves and the life that spins around us. Order. Focus. Energy. These are the by-products of solitude.

(C) *Solitude Lets Us Notice Detail.* When I find time to be alone, that state is not "dumbness," but a receptive attitude which Joseph Pieper, in his famous essay on *Leisure, the Basis of Culture,* defines as "not only the occasion but also the capacity for steeping oneself in the whole of creation."

Stillness allows us to attend to detail: the detail of our own lives, the detail of other persons' lives, the detail of all forms of life around us. This attention to detail is an effort we are not energized to expend unless the waves stop lapping up around our dailyness, but Annie Dillard, Pulitzer Prize winning author of *Pilgrim at Tinker Creek,* begs us to take time to notice, to look. "Look . . . at practically anything—the coot's foot, the mantis's face, a banana, the human ear—and see that not only did the creator create everything, but he's apt to create anything. He'll stop at nothing."[47]

Several years ago, novelist Jessamyn West took off in a travel trailer for a three month stay in the Colorado River backwoods. She documented her journey in a book called *Hide and Seek: A Continuing Journey.*[48]

Of all the things that West learned from her experience, what surprised her most was that ". . . solitude, like a drug, can be addictive. The more you have it, the more you want it." Like Annie Dillard, she unravelled new mysteries in her solitude. For Jessamyn West, "solitude is an unending colloquy between you and yourself and such persons as inhabit your memory and imagination." Persons who were blurs and not appreciated for their specialness, were now individually cherished.

That exhilarating discovery, as well as solitude's benefits of productivity, balance and perspective, combine to prompt a steady stream of people to find time for it.

I ended this section with the comments of Jessamyn *West,* and I began it with gratitude to the *East.* I like what that says, symbolically, about the wholeness of the need and experience of solitude. The truth is, after all, just this: the one journey that ultimately matters is the journey inward. To reach deep within one's self is to know peace and the presence of God. To refuse that adventure is to be disoriented and away from home for the duration of one's life.

The East is very wise and prudent in its instruction and direction. Fortunately, for each of us, there is even more to learn—with patience and gentleness—from our brothers and sisters of another culture and continent.

Some Concluding Comments

I was invited in these pages to address the topic, "Prayer: The Response of the Contemporary Christian," and I would rest more peacefully if I knew that I left with you the distinct impression that there is no such thing as "the" response to prayer. The truth of the matter is that there are as many responses to prayer—contemporary or otherwise—as there are persons. "Souls are never dittos," Friedrich von Hugel wrote to his niece, Gwendolyn Greene. "Genuine prayer," wrote Mark Gibbard, "is exactly the opposite of being ironed out into a pious uniformity."[49] "Nor is it much good picking up ideas, one here, one there, and stirring them all up together."[50] Thus, the prayer of Dorothy Day at Mary House on the Bowery had its own form, as did Dag Hammarskjold's intense response to God at the United Nations. For all the sameness of the prayer experience, it must be admitted that Teilhard de Chardin's relationship to Christ was different from Martin Luther King, Jr's. And, so it should be. "Since prayer is the relation between one particular (person) and God," Carlo Carretto says, "it is different for every (person)."[51] It is different for you. It is different for me. There is a delightful breath of fresh air and freedom in Thomas Merton's observation: "How do you expect to arrive at the end of your journey if you take the road to another (person's) city?"[52]

We must each find our own way, that much we know for certain. But, we also know that others have gone before us, struggling to remain faithful to the human, carving out their responses to a God who pursued them as he pursues each of us—tenderly and relentlessly. We are in good company in coming to grips with our identity in Christ along with other sisters and brothers who, each in her or his way, might say with Dag Hammarskjold:

> For all that has been—thanks!
> To all that shall be—yes![53]

NOTES

[1] See William Johnston, *Christian Zen: A Way of Meditation* (N.Y.: Harper & Row, 1979 Revised Edition), pp. 45-46: "Terminology about acquired and infused contemplation, about ordinary and extraordinary prayer, about *gratia gratis data* and *gratia gratum faciens*—all these complications can quietly and conveniently be dropped. They aren't really necessary, because the experience itself is frightfully simple and uncomplicated. In my opinion we could even dispense with the word contemplation and put in its place 'Christian samadhi.' Besides, contemplation is a Latin word, translation of the Greek *theoria*. Must Christians forever stick to the Hellenistic vocabulary?"

[2] Dag Hammarskjold, *Markings* (New York: Alfred A. Knopf, 1961), p. 205.

[3] Karl Rahner writes: "Mysticism . . . occurs within the framework of normal graces and within the experience of faith. To this extent, those who

insist that mystical experience is not specifically different from the ordinary
grace of life (as such) are certainly right." *Encyclopedia of Theology,* ed. Karl
Rahner (London: Burns and Oates, 1975), p. 1010.

⁴ Thomas Merton, *What is Contemplation?* (Springfield, Illinois: Templegate
Publishers, 1950), p. 11.

⁵ Richard J. Foster, *Celebration of Discipline* (New York: Harper and Row,
1978), p. 1.

⁶ Gerald O'Collins, *The Second Journey* (New York: Paulist Press, 1978), p.
77.

⁷ On the subject of the mid-life journey, references most helpful include:
James Fowler and Sam Keen, *Life Maps: Conversations on the Journey of Faith,* ed.
J. Berryman (Waco, Texas: Word Books, 1978); Roger Gould, *Transformations:
Growth and Change in Adult Life* (New York: Simon and Schuster, 1978); James
E. Loder, *The Transforming Moment* (New York: Harper & Row, 1981); Bernice
Neugarten, "Adult Personality: Toward a Psychology of the Life Cycle," in
Readings in Adult Psychology: Contemporary Perspectives, ed. L. Allman and D. Jaffe
(New York: Harper & Row, 1977), pp. 41-48; Evelyn and James D. White-
head, *Christian Life Patterns: The Psychological Challenges and Religious Invitation of
Adult Life* (New York: Doubleday, 1979).

⁸ See Kenneth Leech, *Soul Friend* (London: Seldon Press, 1977).

⁹ *Ibid.,* p. 32.

¹⁰ A favorite expression of C.S. Lewis. See his *Letters to Malcolm: Chiefly on
Prayer* (New York: Harcourt, Brace, Jovanovich, 1964).

¹¹ Leech, *op. cit.,* p. 33.

¹² Bernard Lonergan, S.J., *Method in Theology* (London: Darton, Longman
and Todd, 1972), pp. 105-106.

¹³ *Ibid.*

¹⁴ Teilhard's vocabulary is helpfully explained in the glossary in Vernon
Sproxton's *Teilhard de Chardin* (London: SCM Press), p. 123.

¹⁵ Pierre Teilhard de Chardin, *The Divine Milieu* (New York: Harper and
Row, 1960), p. 64.

¹⁶ Teresa of Avila wrote of precisely this integration: "We should desire and
engage in prayer, not for our enjoyment, but for the sake of acquiring this
strength which fits us for service. Let us not try to walk along an untrodden
path, or at the best we shall waste our time: it would certainly be a novel idea to
think of receiving these favours from God through any other means than those
used by Him and all his saints. Let us not even consider such a thing: believe
me, Martha and Mary must work together when they offer the Lord lodging,
and must have Him ever with them, and they must not entertain Him badly
and give him nothing to eat. And how can Mary give Him anything, seated as
she is at His feet, unless her sister helps her?" Teresa of Avila, *Interior Castle,*
translated and edited by E. Allison Peers (New York: Doubleday, 1961 edition), p. 231.

¹⁷ Mark Gibbard, *Twentieth Century Men of Prayer* (Naperville, Ill.: SCM
Press, 1974), p. 72.

¹⁸ Thomas Merton, *Conjectures of a Guilty Bystander* (London: Burns & Oates,
1968), pp. 140-41.

¹⁹ "I . . . was overwhelmed by the misery of the world." Henri J.M.
Nouwen, *Genesee Diary* (New York: Doubleday, 1976), p. 147.

²⁰ Pierre Teilhard de Chardin, *Hymn of the Universe* (New York: Harper and
Row, 1965), p. 19.

²¹ William Johnston, *The Inner Eye of Love* (New York: Harper and Row,
1978), pp. 174-75.

²² René Voillaume, *Seeds of the Desert* (London: Burns and Oates, 1955), p.
323.

²³ Kenneth Leech, *True Prayer* (New York: Harper and Row, 1980), p. 85.

²⁴ John Eudes Bamberger, O.C.S.O., in the Preface to Henri Nouwen's *Thomas Merton: Contemplative Critic* (New York: Harper and Row, 1981), p. ix.
²⁵ William Miller, *A Harsh and Dreadful Love* (New York: Doubleday Image Book, 1973), p. 25, for this quote from *The Brothers Karamazov*.
²⁶ "Shalom, Dorothy," *National Catholic Reporter*, 12 December 1980, p. 1.
²⁷ Dorothy Sölle, *Revolutionary Patience* (New York: Orbis Books, 1977), p. 73.
²⁸ Segundo Galilea, *Following Jesus*, trans. Sister Helen Philips, M.M. (New York: Orbis Books, 1981 English Translation), p. 32.
²⁹ From an address of Archbishop Hunthausen in "The Shepherds Speak" series at St. James Cathedral, Brooklyn, on May 16, 1982.
³⁰ On this subject of dreams and their interpretation, I am especially indebted to Erich Fromm, *The Forgotten Language: An Introduction to the Understanding of Dreams, Fairy Tales and Myths* (New York: 1961, 1951); C.G. Jung, *Memories, Dreams, Reflections*, recorded and edited by Aniela Jaffe (New York: Pantheon Books, 1963); and Maria F. Mahoney, *The Meaning in Dreams and Dreaming* (Secaucus, New Jersey: The Citadel Press, 1976).
³¹ See the *Rite of Penance, 1974*, International Committee on English in the Liturgy, Inc. (Washington, D.C.: USCC Publications Office, 1975).
³² John Claypool, "The Event of Forgiveness," Broadway Baptist Church Sermons, Fort Worth, Texas, XII, No. 23, October 14, 1973:4.
³³ Richard Foster, *op. cit.*, p. 130.
³⁴ *Ibid.*, pp. 131-32.
³⁵ From an unpublished manuscript of Morton Kelsey submitted as a conference study paper to the Advisory Board of the Academy of Spiritual Formation at their May 6-7, 1982, meeting in Nashville, Tennessee.
³⁶ *Ibid.*
³⁷ In addition to innumerable articles, the books of Thomas Merton that I have found most helpful in this area of indebtedness to the East are: *The Asian Journal of Thomas Merton*, ed. Naomi Burton, Brother Patrick Hart and James Laughlin (New York: New Directions, 1973); *Mystics and Zen Masters* (New York: Farrar, Straus and Giroux, 1967); *The Way of Chuang Tzu* (New York: New Directions, 1965); and *Zen and the Birds of Appetite* (New York: New Directions, 1968).
³⁸ I am grateful to William Johnston for authoring the following: *The Inner Eye of Love* (New York: Harper and Row, 1978); *The Mirror Mind* (New York: Harper and Row, 1981); *Silent Music* (New York: Harper and Row, 1974); and *The Still Point* (New York: Fordham University Press, 1970).
³⁹ I feel kinship with these lines of Thomas Merton, written in his notes before a conference in Calcutta: "I have left my monastery to come here not just as a research scholar or even as an author. I come as a pilgrim who is anxious to obtain not just information, not just 'facts' about other monastic traditions, but to drink from ancient sources of monastic vision and experience." Thomas Merton, *The Asian Journal of Thomas Merton*, p. 4.
⁴⁰ For the distinctions between Zen and Zen Buddhism, I am indebted to William Johnston and his book, *Christian Zen: A Way of Meditation* (New York: Harper, reprinted 1979), especially pp. 33-38.
⁴¹ Mother Teresa, "The Poor in Our Midst," in *New Covenant* (Ann Arbor, Michigan, January 1977).
⁴² William Johnston, *Silent Music*, p. 36.
⁴³ *Apophthegmata Patrum*, Poemen 27; pg 65:329A.
⁴⁴ Dag Hammarskjold, *Markings*, p. xxi.
⁴⁵ Richard Foster, *op. cit.*, p. 93.
⁴⁶ Anne Morrow Lindbergh, *Gift from the Sea* (New York: Random House, A Vintage Book, 1965).
⁴⁷ Annie Dillard, *Pilgrim at Tinker Creek* (New York: Bantam, 1978), p. 72.

[48] Jessamyn West, *Hide and Seek: A Continuing Journey* (New York: Harcourt, Brace, Jovanovich, 1973), quoted by Susan A. Muto, in *A Practical Guide to Spiritual Reading* (Denville, New Jersey: Dimension Books, 1976), pp. 140-41.

[49] Mark Gibbard, *op. cit.*, p. 110. I am indebted to Father Gibbard for his insights on the uniqueness of the prayer experience in these concluding remarks.

[50] *Ibid.*, p. 111.

[51] Carlo Carretto, *Letters from the Desert* (London: Darton, Longman & Todd, 1972), p. 36.

[52] Thomas Merton, *New Seeds of Contemplation* (London: Burns & Oates, 1972), p. 76.

[53] Hammarskjold, *op. cit.*, p. 87.

Peace and Justice in the Nuclear Age

Richard McSorley, S.J.

What we do expresses what we believe better than our words. Take our belief in God; believe we do—and yet, we kill, enslave, and oppress. So, do we really believe in God? I can deceive myself and say I do. I pray; I go to Mass, but my God becomes one who accepts what I do—even in my thoughts as I believe in a God that murders, enslaves, and oppresses. I make my own God in my own image and say I believe in God. No doubt this is possible with good conscience, but St. John says, "If anyone says, 'My love is fixed on God,' yet hates his brother, he is a liar" (1 John 9:20). St. James says, "What good is it to profess faith without practicing it?" (James 2:14). He answers, "Faith that does nothing in practice. It is thoroughly lifeless" (James 2:17).

Why is it that faith shows itself in action?

First, action comes from faith. I once had a college student who was trying to prove God's existence from mathematics. His parents were store keepers. They spent sixteen hours a day in their store. The son was convinced they did not believe in God because they were so busy with their store. He did not see any sign of belief in God in their lives, although they said they believed. He was judging by what they did. He saw his parents as atheists and tried to prove them wrong by mathematics.

A second reason faith shows itself in action is failure to act as we believe changes belief: a draft resister who came to me during the Vietnam war asked, "Can I be a conscientious objector even though I am not a practicing Catholic?"

I asked, "What do you mean by 'practicing Catholic'?"

"Well, I don't go to church."

"Do you believe that life is sacred?"

"Yes."

"Do you believe in killing others?"

"No."

"Which do you think Jesus would consider a practicing Catholic, one who goes to Mass and kills, or one who does not go to Mass but for conscience' sake refuses to kill. If Jesus had to choose, which of the two would he consider a 'practicing Catholic'?"

"I guess the one who would not kill."

Another example was a man who left his wife after twenty-five years of marriage. He told me, "I believe in God, but not in marriage."

I pointed out to him that God instituted marriage.

A year later I met him and asked how things were going.

"I have solved my problem. I no longer believe in God." He said he did away with his belief in God to avoid the conflict in his life of belief and practice.

He may be more consistent than the nuclear submarine captain who told me, "I am for peace."

It is in the light of this relationship of faith to actions, theory to practice, that I propose to look at the relationship of the gospel of peace to nuclear age technology. The threat of thermo-nuclear destruction that faces all of us is bringing many to a new understanding of the gospel of peace. The nuclear technology we are building is intimately related to what we believe, the gospel. Both an analysis of what nuclear technology is and what the gospel says about peace may help us to grow in the practice of peacemaking.

The Gospel of Peace.

One way to get a focus on what the gospel says is to seriously ask and answer the question, "Does the New Testament approve of war?"

A person who knew nothing about Christ but who decided to discover what Christ taught by observing the way Christians live might decide that Christ taught as follows:

Blessed are the rich for theirs is the kingdom of God.

Blessed are the violent for they shall possess the land.

Blessed are those who afflict others, they shall be comforted.

Blessed are those who hunger and thirst for power, they will be filled.

Blessed are the merciless, they will get ahead.

Blessed are the war-makers, they are God's children.

Blessed are you when men honor you and say all manner of praise about you, for your reward is also great in heaven.

In like manner from the way Christians prepare to kill and have killed each other through the centuries you would expect to find that the gospel is a book of war, or at least teaches Christians to hate and kill. This contradiction between theory and practice has gone on so long that even the theory has become obscured and even faded from the sight of many people. Rarely do you hear a sermon on the relation of the gospel to war. Few Christians ask themselves the question, "Does the gospel approve of war?" The answer to that question is presumed to be "Yes," without any serious look at the gospel because the massive "Yes" of Christian practice has obscured the gospel message.

For these and other reasons it is important to seriously ask and answer the question, "Does the New Testament approve of war?"

To answer that question maybe the clearest way is to look at what the New Testament says about war and peace.

A few definitions are needed: "New Testament," as used here, means only the gospels, epistles, Acts of the Apostles and Apocalypse: not the books of the Old Testament. They need their own special treatment which I discuss in my book, *The New Testament Basis of Peacemaking.*

When I ask the question, "Does the New Testament approve of war?," I am not asking, "Does the New Testament approve of a police force?," or "Does the New Testament approve of any kind of violence?" That is a different question and will be answered afterwards. But, first the question on "war."

"War," as I use it, is "inter-group lethal conflict." "War" is used in many ways, "war on poverty," a bloodless coup d'état, the occupation of the Dominican Republic by the United States marines without bloodshed, John Brown's raid at Harper's Ferry to free the slaves. Even some of these might be "inter-group lethal conflict." So, to clearly say what I mean by war I put it this way. "Inter-group lethal conflict" with these characteristics:

1) Much killing.

2) A momentum of its own that carries both sides to acts of savagery unthought of at the beginning of the war. Two outstanding examples of this in World War II are the destruction of Coventry by the Germans and the atomic bombing of Hiroshima and Nagasaki by the United States.

3) Psychological and spiritual mobilization of group against group.

The more clearly and fully the question is developed the more obviously and surely the answer appears. "No, the New Testament does not approve of anything defined like that."

How can I best give the answer from the New Testament? An examination of the concepts and the texts of the New Testament follows.

Reasons the New Testament Does Not Approve of War.

Rather than start with individual texts I will present five basic principles taught in the New Testament. These principles are not marginal or superficial aspects of the New Testament, but are so basic that, were they denied, the New Testament itself would be denied.

First Principle—Love

Love is one of the most misused words in the world today. It is the central message of the New Testament. Jesus summarized his entire teaching in the command, "Love God and your neighbor." He chose love as the mark differentiating his followers from others. This love was all embracing. It included all, even enemies. "Love your enemies and pray for those who persecute you" (Matt 5:44). "Do not resist one who is evil" (Matt 5:39).

What does this mean and how is it applied to war? It means that my attitude towards my neighbor should not be determined by the damage done to me, or that might be done to me. It means I must respond in terms of the good of the person or group involved. It is not a principle of do-nothing-under-attack, but an active effort to express Divine Love by seeking the good of the enemy.

Active love is the response Jesus wants us to have even towards our enemies. Our love is to be independent of the attitude of the other person. We are to love simply because God wants us to reveal ourselves as true sons and daughters of our heavenly Father by this love.

"For if you love those who love you, what reward have you? Do not even the tax collectors do the same? And if you salute only your brethren what more are you doing than others? Do not even the Gentiles do the same?" (Matt 5:46-48). In Jesus' teaching all thought of reciprocity is excluded. We are not asked to love the Soviets because they love us, but because God loves us. When Jesus preached the sermon on the mount, he asked his followers to lead a certain way of life independently of what others might do. His words, "Blessed are you when men revile you and persecute you and utter all kinds of evil against you falsely on my account" (Matt 5:11), make it clear that there is no reciprocity.

The promise of persecution and the command to "love your enemies" both illustrate the universality of the love Christ commands. This rules out killing one person to protect others—I can not exclude even one person from my love. Such a love would not be universal. The common argument used to defend war, "We kill these people to defend others," has no foundation in the gospel. It violates the command of universal love. To comply with the law of universality you have to argue that in the act of killing you were showing love to the person you were killing. That seems impossible to me—impossible and contradictory.

Some who defend war as compatible with Christian love argue that it is possible to kill and destroy without feeling any hatred for the enemy.

One response to this is that the absence of hate is not what the gospel asks. What it asks is positive, active love. Is it more virtuous to kill without hate than to kill with hate? The blinding power of hate may make killing in hate less culpable before God, than a cold-blooded murder.

A second response is that any use of force by a Christian is subject to conditions imposed by the gospel:

1) Force can never be a substitute for the obligation of love.

2) Any use of force makes love more difficult.

3) Any use of force that is compatible with the gospel must be preparatory to and directed towards love for the person against whom the force is used. An example would be spanking a child with a few light taps that do no physical damage but instruct the child about the danger of playing in the street.

4) If the use of force is such that it makes any appeal to love impossible, then a Christian can never resort to it—for instance, spanking a child to death.

War does not fulfill these conditions. War kills. Death puts the person wholly beyond the reach of human love. The gospel calls for personal love. Modern warfare, with its long distance lethal technology, is so impersonal that any kind of personal love relationship with the enemy is next to impossible. War poisons personal relationships by lying, trickery and distrust of the enemy simply because he/she is an enemy. Even the training for war illustrates this. It is a training in depersonalization of both self and the enemy.

Training puts all in the same uniform, teaches all to march, to turn, to reverse, to count steps, to count numbers, to eat, sleep, and to go when, where, and how you are ordered to.

It is a training in taking orders, even though they are monstrous and stupid, until you get to a point where you see yourself as a cog in the military machine. At that point you obey orders without questions, even orders to kill. All of your training aims at helping you to obey without thought, without question. You no longer think of yourself as responsible for what you do. You no longer think of the target you shoot at as a person. You think of a person as a target, an obstacle, an enemy, or a demon. The training in depersonalization prepares you to kill.

War is contrary to the gospel because war includes much killing, and killing leaves no room for the all embracing love-command.

Some who argue that the New Testament approves of war confuse police action with war. They are not the same.

Police action may escalate to a point where it is similar to war, especially in time of war. Ordinarily there are clear patterns of difference. While the police act within a limited area—their own country, the military move into other countries. While the police aim to arrest, the military aim to kill or destroy individuals, groups and even whole areas. While police use small weapons, and generally non-lethal weapons, the military use lethal weapons of mass destructive capacity. While police operate according to the law of their country, the military operate in the jungle of international affairs.

Even if you believe that police action in general for the sake of public order is compatible with the gospel, police action is different enough from war that there is no contradiction in accepting one and rejecting the other. Where police action becomes lethal, it becomes more like war and becomes subject to the same disapproval as war.

Second Principle—God, Our Father-Mother

The New Testament teaches there is only one God. God is our Father. We are all Children of God. Because of this we ought to act towards each other as brothers and sisters.

This is the teaching underlying the command, "Love one another." This is the reason Jesus can summarize our relation to God and to each other in the love-command.

It is the basic theology that opposes war. This is the rock on which the Christian who opposes war can stand. I may not know all the intricacies of foreign policies or all the complexities of military strategies. What I do know is that there is only one God, and that we are all God's Children. If foreign policy and military strategy can not be reconciled with this belief, then I can not accept them.

Jesus taught us to pray with the words, "Our Father." Throughout his teaching he speaks of the Father's love for us. To deny that we are brothers and sisters to each other is a kind of implicit atheism. It denies God's existence as our common source of being.

There is quite a difference in believing that all humans are my brothers and sisters and believing that some are and some are not. If I believe that some are not God's children, maybe I can kill them and please God: maybe I am better than they are because I am God's child and they are not. The common bond between militarism and racism is evident here.

Prayer reflects belief. Prayer grows out of beliefs and indicates what beliefs I hold. My prayer will be quite different when I believe we are all God's children and when I do not.

For Christians who believe that Christ is our brother, our relationship to each other as brother and sister is also an expression of our belief in and relation to Christ as our brother and as God Incarnate. Through the Incarnation (God as man in human form) we are children of God because, if Jesus is our brother, Jesus' Father is our Father too. Denial of our brotherhood, sisterhood, is also an implicit denial of the Incarnation.

Third Principle—The Almost Infinite Value of the Human Person

The redemption of each person in Christ's blood gives each one an almost infinite value. Christ's death is not only a measure of God's love for us, but also a measure of our value in God's eyes—the death through crucifixion of His Son Jesus, that is our value. It is the Christian belief that God so loved each one of us that, if I were the only person in the universe, he would have given his life for me alone. The death of God on the cross is the cost of our salvation and of our individual worth. War denies all this with its depersonalization, its subordination of human life to the needs of the state, or to military necessity.

Fourth Principle—Means and Ends Relationship

To claim that war, even for a just cause, can be just, irrespective of the means employed, is possible only on the assumption that the end justifies the means. To hold that military necessity knows no law or that the end justifies the means is a betrayal of Christian principle. Jacques Maritain writes:

> Nothing is more terrible than to see evil barbarous means employed by men claiming to act in the name of Christian order. . . . The character of the end is already predetermined in the means. It is a truth inscribed in the very nature of things, that Christianity will recreate itself by Christian means, or it will perish completely.[1]

The gospel teaches that means and ends are compatible. The goal of the gospel is union with God. The means are compatible with it, love of God and others, and so compatible that means and end are convertible. Love is union with God. Union with God is love. All the varied gospel ways of manifesting love—faith, forgiveness, poverty, hope, suffering, and service of others—are compatible with union with God.

This is quite opposite to the military method. There, the means and end are contradictory. "Saving" is said to be done by killing and destroying. This is illustrated in the prayer at the christening of a nuclear submarine, "God bless this submarine, may it be an instrument of peace." A submarine with nuclear weapons is seen as a means of peace. Even the act of using the term "christening" in sending a warship underway is a kind of blasphemy. Christening is for people, and is a sign of God's grace.

Armies try to achieve peace through war, order through chaos, security through violence, the reign of law through lawlessness; to preserve honor by dishonorable acts: in the end they say they save by destroying. This was actually voiced by the United States officer at Ben Tre, Vietnam, "We had to destroy the village in order to save it."

Mark Twain's famous War Prayer illustrates how a prayer for victory is also a prayer that God will help us kill, make widows and orphans, and make our enemies hungry and homeless.

Mark Twain says that when we pray to God for victory, we pray to take the bodies of our enemy's soldiers and tear them "to bloody shreds with our shells." We pray to God to "help us to lay waste their humble hopes with a hurricane of fire."

We pray to God to "help us to turn them out roofless with their little children to wander unfriended the wastes of their desolated land."

When means and goal are comparable and contradictory, the means tend to become the end, as they do in this prayer.

Gandhi said, "The creator has given us control (and that too, very limited) over means, none over the end. Realization of the goal is in exact proportion to that of the means. This is a proposition that admits of no exception."[2]

In Jesus' teaching means and ends are always compatible. "You will know them by their fruits. Are grapes gathered from thorns, or figs from thistles?"

When the means is not only incompatible with the goal but contradictory to it, both reasons separate it from the gospel. The evil is not justified by the end envisaged.

The fruits of war are horror, death, suffering, moral degradation, arson, rape, lying, murder and more war. There are things worse than war, and war brings every one of them.

Dorothy Day of *The Catholic Worker* says there is no need of any special theology of peace. You just need to look at what the gospel asks and what war does. The gospel asks that we feed the hungry, give drink to the thirsty, clothe the naked, welcome the homeless, visit the prisoner, and perform the works of mercy. War does all the opposite. It makes my neighbor hungry, thirsty, homeless, a prisoner and sick. The gospel asks us to take up our cross. War asks us to lay the cross of suffering on others.

Jesus refused to establish his kingdom by means suggested by the devil and contrary to his Father's plan. The devil asked him to prove that he was the Messiah by changing stones to bread and by falling down from the top of the temple without being hurt. Both would be spectacular acts of power: far different from dying on the cross as a redemptive sacrifice. Jesus refused actions that were incompatible with his Father's plan for the Messiah. The devil promised him all the kingdoms of the earth if "bowing down you will adore me." Jesus ordered Satan, "Be gone!" The means suggested by the devil were not compatible with his Father's plan but contradictory to it.

Military means (killing and destroying) is a type of idolatry. It is worshipping a false god, the God of war—Mars. We trust in our arms, not God. We do not trust in God's way of love, of redemptive suffering. We think we will get the peace—that only God can give—without God's help and even in contradiction to God's plan. In fact, we will get peace with Satan's help and advice. We yield to the temptation that Christ rejected. We will do it our way. We will put our talents, our resources, our youth, our treasures at the service of the god of war, not at the service of the God of love. The result that we get out of this is war. Our means and end become compatible and convertible.

Fifth Principle—Imitation of Christ

For the Christian the best description of holiness is "imitation of Christ." Other descriptions, like "doing God's will," "following the light," "living perfectly," are all included in imitation of Christ. Unlike an abstract definition, Christ's life reaches us on every level: intellectual, physical, emotional and spiritual. His life is not just words, or a book; it is a living example. Any questions we might have about a text of scripture—does it approve war or not?—should be resolved by comparing it with the example of Christ's life. For example, "Render unto Caesar the things that are Caesar's." Does this mean that we should kill when Caesar says "Kill"? Is it not clear from Jesus' life and especially from His death that even when Caesar killed him, Jesus would not defend himself? We need not imagine what Christ would do if asked to push the button that would send a nuclear weapon to kill millions. We have the example of his life. He was and is a pacifist, a peacemaker. He came to reconcile us to the Father (Eph. 2:12-19). Because of him we are no longer Jew and Gentile but one people. He has broken the barriers that separated us and has reconciled us to God and to each other. He has done this by the wood of the cross (Eph. 2:16).

Here we have the definition of peace. Peace is reconciliation among God, myself and my neighbor. Peace is always three-sided: God, self and neighbor. Peace can never leave God out, nor can there be any peace with God and myself if I leave my neighbor out. Peace, like love, simultaneously includes God and neighbor.

For the Christian, Christ is the peacemaker, the reconciler. His method is the cross: accepting suffering with love, not inflicting it on others. The invitation of the gospel to love is entirely contradictory to the use of military force. Jesus wins love by trust and suffering service. The military achieve their goal by force, fear and death. Christ's way of life, Christ's example, was not military. It was a way of pacifist-peacemaking, a way of making peace through the cross, through redemptive love.

Jesus' whole life showed the pattern of using peaceful, non-coercive means to attain his end, the Kingdom of God on earth. Born without prestige, in a stable, he lived most of his life unknown in a small town. He chose poor fishermen as his apostles, not the great and powerful. He called himself the "good shepherd," not a general. "I am the true vine" (John 15:1), he said. His spirit appeared in the form of a dove, not a hawk or an eagle. His three years of public life were spent as a wandering street preacher without a place to lay his head. His program for action (Matt 5:1-8), blessing the poor, the gentle, the afflicted, those hungry for justice, being merciful, peacemaking, singlehearted, persecuted, also described his own life. His death on the cross as a condemned criminal, not a conquering general, completed and reenforced the pattern of his life. His way of bringing peace was not the sword, not physical force, but the appeal of a lover suffering for the beloved, accompanied by divine powers that made suffering and death into joy and life. The military system of getting your way through death and destruction leaves no room for Divine power that works through the paradox of saving life through losing your own, exemplified in Christ's life and death.

His life is the "way" God teaches us to live. It is entirely opposed to the way of war.

Jesus summarized his life and teaching in these words, "Love your enemies!" That still is our theory and our faith. But, it has not been our practice. By and large we have not followed Jesus' way of peace since the first three centuries when Christians refused to join the army or to kill because of their faith.

Paradoxically, it is the nuclear age which is helping us return to our peace-faith because we are beginning to see in an analysis of nuclear technology that we can not hope for peace in that direction. In the light of that technology we see how far we have gone from the gospel of peace which we still say is what we believe.

Nuclear Technology.

If we seriously considered the destructive force of nuclear weapons, we would not look on them as a way to securing peace. This would be a big change in our thinking. Einstein noted this. He said, "The splitting of the atom has changed everything save our modes of thinking and thus we drift toward unparalleled catastrophe."

To understand the power of nuclear weapons, compare them with the big bombs of World War II. A World War II blockbuster was the equivalent of a ton of TNT in explosive force. A large air raid was equivalent to one thousand tons of TNT. An entire air raid like that is twenty times smaller than the small nuclear weapon dropped on Hiroshima. Since that bomb was equivalent to twenty thousand tons, the Hiroshima bomb is a baby in the atomic weapon family.

The Hiroshima bomb size has to be multiplied by fifty to equal the size of a one-megaton bomb. "Megaton" is one of the new words coined to describe a million tons of TNT equivalent, and megatonnage has no theoretical upper limit.

The early H-bomb in 1952 was a three-megaton weapon, the equivalent of three million tons of TNT in destructive power. A later H-bomb, tested by the Soviet Union in 1961, was fifty-seven megatons. It is difficult to imagine what this means: the strength of such an H-bomb is equivalent to the explosive power of a one thousand ton World War II air raid, continued every day for one hundred fifty-six years!

When you consider that these weapons can be carried in airplanes traveling faster than sound, delivered in missiles or from submarines that remain at the bottom of the sea, the dimension of danger increases. Some idea of what nuclear war would be like can be obtained by looking at what one weapon can destroy. Multiply that destruction by the number of weapons likely to be used. This gives you a picture of the basic destruction likely in World War III.

What would a twenty-megaton nuclear bomb do if it exploded in the heart of New York City? It is important to consider the bomb in relation to a city for two reasons. First, the likely target of these bombs is cities. Second, eighty per cent of the American people live in cities. We are an urban population. It is an irony of fate that the most urban population in the world has developed the weapons that can destroy cities. The first result of a twenty-megaton bomb dropped on midtown Manhattan would be death. The total number of people killed would be about ten times the total number of battle deaths that the United States has suffered throughout all its history, that is, from the American Revolution through Vietnam. The estimated deaths would be six million of New York's eight million people and another million dead beyond the city limits.

Blast Effect

A twenty-megaton bomb has "more destructive power than a mountain of TNT four times the height of the Empire State Building . . . more . . . than a caravan of one million trucks each carrying 20,000 pounds of TNT."[3] Its blast would make a hole in solid rock deep enough to contain a twenty-story building, and the hole would be half a mile wide. The detonation would set a huge pressure wave in motion. This would roar out from the explosion center as a shock front, backed by winds moving at over one thousand miles per hour.

Behind the pressure front, a vast vacuum would be created. Into this, the winds from the surrounding area would rush as the pressure diminished. Structures not smashed by the shock front might be toppled by the winds sucked in by the vacuum from the opposite direction.

Most casualties in New York City would come from falling buildings and flying objects. Some people would be killed by being blown against walls and hard objects. "Trucks would be lifted and thrown like grotesque Molotov cocktails to spew gasoline, oil and automotive shrapnel onto and into everything in their path. In an instant most underground gasoline and oil tanks would rupture and explode within the blast area."[4]

Within a ten-mile radius from the center, the area of lethal or severe blast, basement shelters would be buried. All living things in the subway systems would die. Frame houses and two-story brick buildings would be destroyed. "Few, if any, of New York City's approximately 2,500,000 dwelling units would provide adequate shelter for survivors, even if everything were not consumed by fires."[5]

The blast would destroy hospitals, rupture water mains, and para-lyze transportation. The winds from the blast would fan the fury of the fires to follow it.

Firestorm

After the incandescent flash across the sky, a fireball as hot as the sun and many times brighter would begin to rise from the earth. It would be four and a half miles across. Like a hot air balloon, it would rise to a height of twenty miles, emitting visible and invisible radiation and scorching the countryside. Clothing on people twenty miles away would burst into flame; paper and similar material would pass their combustion point at thirty-seven miles. "People about 40 miles away would suffer first degree burns."[6]

A sea of fire would roll and burn within a radius extending thirty-seven miles from the center. And, as far away as three hundred miles from the blast center retinal damage might be inflicted on those who looked at the fire wall. (Rabbits at that distance from the United States Pacific tests of smaller bombs had their eyes burned by the flash of the bomb.) Closer to the fire center less combustible materials like asphalt would blaze.

Radiation

Blast effects and even some of the fireball effects are familiar from past wars. Their size and power are increased with nuclear weapons. Radiation effect, however, is entirely new and different.

A ground burst gives off more radioactive fallout than an air burst. The reason is that the material in the crater created by the blast is vaporized, and the same is true of many objects touched by the fireball. In the case of a twenty-megaton bomb dropped on New York City, the crater would be more than six hundred feet deep and one and a half miles across. The vaporized material would be carried into the upper atmosphere and then fall according to wind currents as radioactive particles. The heavy material falls first, the lighter drifts farther before falling to the ground.

Radiation damage may result from exposure to these particles. Long-range injury is incurred by the body's becoming a despository of radioactive materials. Radiation damage is measured in roentgen units. One roentgen is enough to damage human cells. The number of roentgens necessary to kill fifty per cent of the humans exposed is four hundred fifty roentgens.

Large doses of two thousand or three thousand roentgens kill by paralyzing the central nervous system. Doses of about fifteen hundred roentgens kill by producing fatal gastrointestinal disorders. Below fifteen hundred units the roentgen dosage affects the blood system. It decreases the oxygen, white blood cells, and the ability of the blood to clot. This may explain blue or purple patches beneath the skin of radiation patients.

Fallout from a twenty-megaton ground burst on New York City would cover an area of about forty-eight hundred square miles, depending on the wind. If the wind blew east, this would include Connecticut and the Cape Cod area. In this area the roentgen dosage would be twenty-one hundred units by the end of the second day and then would decline. During these two days, exposed persons would probably die. But, the air would remain lethal to fifty per cent of the population for at least the next twelve days, perhaps for as long as two months. For twelve days the dosage would be five hundred seventy-five roentgens. Afterward, it would decline, but one hundred roentgens would continue to exist during the next ten months.

The only way that the population could adequately protect itself would be to have three feet of dirt or two feet of concrete between itself and the radiation for the period of danger. Those who emerged from shelters would return to a different world. Food, air and water would be poisoned, and essential life support systems would be gone. The new ecology would support bacteria, viruses, and disease-bearing insects, much more resistant to radiation than humans, which would mutate, adapt, and multiply in extremely virulent forms. Plagues of unprecedented nature and of diseases yet unknown would make life an insupportable burden. For those who survived these horrors cancer and leukemia would become rampant.

Any major nuclear exchange would affect the ozone layer that protects the earth from the harmful ultraviolet radiation in sunlight. Without this invisible, and to many of the earth's people, this unknown protective shield, sunlight would be harmful to most living organisms. The ozone layer was a precondition to the development of multicelled plants and animals, and all life forms have evolved under this shield. It is a type of womb for the whole earth, and the living matter on it. Destroying it would impose a permanent state of abortion on this earth. Fred Ilke, former director of the Arms Control and Disarmament Agency and a member of the Reagan Defense Department, said that severe reduction of the ozone layer through nuclear explosions could "shatter the ecological structure that permits man to remain alive on this planet."

All the ensuing ill effects from reduction of the ozone layer are impossible to calculate, but a few possibilities are worth spending some time on to assess their ramifications. One possibility is that, though fur would protect the skin of the earth's animals, they would all become blind. If insects were blinded also, their disorientation would stop the pollination essential for plants to continue. Living organs exposed to the greatest risk would be those at the bottom of the food chain, the unicellular organisms. Elimination of an organism from the food chain can eliminate all the organisms above it in the chain.

Radioactive material is deposited within the bone structure of the body when one breathes contaminated air or eats and drinks radioactive material. This was vividly illustrated in the British tests. The antlers of a deer and the teeth of a sheep became so radioactive that they printed their own image on a photographic plate. The deposit of radioactive strontium 90 and caesium 137 caused the bone structure to act like an internal X-ray machine.

How long contamination from eating or drinking radioactive materials may last can be judged by the United States Navy's announcement of August 11, 1968, that Bikini Atoll is now fit for human habitation. The Navy conducted tests on Bikini in 1946. These carefully limited tests made the atoll unsafe for human life for twenty years, at least. When the people moved back, all was not well. They developed symptoms peculiar to over exposure to radiation. Some of the islanders had to move away again. It was found that radiation had a peculiar tendency to concentrate in parts of the food chain, such as coconuts, and in portions of the earth structure.

Those who survived a ground burst of a heavy nuclear device would be living for weeks, if they lived at all, in a radioactive oven. Every responsible scientist admits that fallout of large megatonnage would leave us with an appalling number of deformities and problems that would multiply through the generations rather than fade away. The devastation of a general nuclear war is simply beyond human imagination.

Lesser Bombs

I have concentrated attention on the twenty megaton weapon since that is a medium-sized one between the one megaton and the fifty-seven megaton weapons which are within our capacity for use. Similar charts of the circle of destruction of a one megaton or a ten megaton blast could easily be laid out. Their destructive capacity is still immense. Twenty bombs of one-megaton size would do more proportionate damage than one twenty-megaton bomb. For example, each one megaton would have a blast area of three to four miles in radius (compared with the ten mile blast radius of the twenty megaton bomb); a firestorm area three to nine miles in radius (compared with the twenty-seven miles for the twenty megaton); and radiation that would start over the six to eighteen mile diameter of the firestorm and blow two hundred miles with the wind (compared with the forty-eight hundred square mile radiation area for a twenty megaton bomb). In addition, the "ones" could be placed according to density of population; the "twenty" would have to hit a single target. The "ones" could be exploded both on the ground and in the air over the same target, or on different targets. The effects of air and ground bursts are different. Air bursts produce thirty to forty per cent more blast and fire damage than ground bursts. A ground burst gives off much more radiation.

Japan, 1945.

Instead of circles and statistics, the effect of nuclear weapons on people tells a more effective story of their destructive power in human terms.

After the markets were open at Hiroshima and the people were on their way to work, a single atom bomb was dropped from a high altitude. The bomb measured only twenty-eight inches by one hundred twenty-eight inches. It floated down on a parachute. At 1,804 feet above the ground it exploded. A picture taken shortly after the explosion shows the devastation: charred human bodies on a desert of wreckage. Our country's official report estimates that sixty-six thousand people were killed and sixty-nine thousand were injured. Other reports put the number of dead closer to one hundred thousand. All this killing in a few minutes!

With this act we became the first nation to drop an atomic weapon on human beings. We are still the only nation to have done so. These two acts of destruction, the bomb at Hiroshima and the second bomb at Nagasaki, may be the most important part of our national heritage in the scale of our influence on the life of this planet.

The bomb was dropped despite the plea of a group of scientists to President Truman that we should not be the first to do this. The argument is sometimes given that we killed all of those people and injured almost twice as many in order to save lives and bring the war to an end. But, this rationalization is without merit.

We could have starved the Japanese war machine by interfering with its supply of fuel. We could have waited! Germany had already surrendered. Victory was assured. As Philip Berrigan points out, President Truman acted against the advice of the best military and civilian leaders in both England and the United States. Those who advised against the use of the bomb included General Eisenhower, Churchill, and the United States Joint Chiefs of Staff—except General Marshall.[7]

The argument that dropping the bomb was necessary to force Japan into ending the war is simply contrary to the facts.

Japan was already asking for peace. One faction in Japan was demanding that its government end the war. Whatever rationalization we might have made for the destruction of Hiroshima was weakened when, three days later, we fried Nagasaki in a nuclear flash.

On August 9 at 11:02 p.m., another B-29 dropped a bomb on the industrial section of Nagasaki, totally destroying the city, killing thirty-nine thousand persons and injuring twenty-five thousand more. This was our report. Other estimates put the casualties higher. A general rule of thumb is that for each death there are twice that number of casualties.

After the detonation, the devastation made Nagasaki look like incinerated Hiroshima. Our argument that we were trying to save lives now seems hollow and empty. Before we weighed the effects of the first bomb and while Japan was still trying to assess it, we struck again. The bombs of Nagasaki and Hiroshima gave us an incarnate example of what the bomb can do to a city.

These were small bombs on relatively small cities, but their effect on the people of Japan, even today, is to make them adverse to any military cooperation with the United States and afraid of the same thing happening again. This is the reason mass protests against American nuclear installations in Japan and against cooperation with the United States in Vietnam strike a resonant chord in the hearts of most Japanese. They have felt the terror of atomic destruction.

Overkill Capacity.

Now we have a basic estimate of the damage that can be done with a single nuclear weapon. Multiply this destruction by the number of weapons that both we and the Soviet Union possess, and you can get a realistic estimate of what these weapons could do.

How many weapons does the United States have? In February of 1968, Secretary McNamara said the United States had forty-five hundred nuclear warheads. That was at the time that I started to write on this subject. Of these forty-five hundred, 656 were ready to be launched from nuclear-powered submarines. The Soviet Union had one thousand nuclear warheads. Secretary McNamara also pointed out with a chart that a total of four hundred megatons is all that is needed to destroy seventy-six per cent of any enemy's industrial capacity. He showed from his table that increasing the number of megatons four times would only increase the amount of industrial capacity destroyed by one per cent.[8]

In other words, with four hundred megatons as the breakoff point for deterring any aggressor, we have ten times more megatons than we need. This is something new in warfare. It used to be that the way to win a war was to develop more or bigger weapons than the enemy. Now, we both have such weapons and so many more than we need that no deterrent advantage comes from more or bigger weapons. In fact, the development of bigger weapons might provoke nuclear war on the part of the power unable to develop more weapons.

"Overkill" is the word that expresses this. It tells of a frustration at the limits of power ("how many times can you kill a man?")— frustration because "more power" is no longer the program for victory. "Overkill" means that we possess the power to totally destroy the Russians, plus the additional power to totally destroy that destruction some forty plus times over. For those among us who would believe in and imagine devils, can we imagine that a devil could devise a more diabolic scheme?

At the SALT (Strategic Arms Limitation) talk of May, 1972, we admitted we had 5,792 warheads ready to go. By the time the SALT agreement ended in 1977, we had almost ten thousand warheads, and the Soviet Union had almost four thousand. Now, we have about thirty thousand nuclear weapons.[9] The Russians have about twenty-thousand. The United States has 9,480 strategic weapons; Russia has 7,868 strategic weapons. We also have twenty-two thousand smaller weapons, and the Russians have ten thousand of these so-called tactical weapons. We continue to make a new nuclear weapon every eight hours.

Another way of understanding the four hundred megatons delivered on the enemy as the outside limit of deterrence is this: The Soviet Union has approximately two hundred cities with a population of one hundred thousand or more. If we delivered one nuclear weapon on each of these cities, we would devastate the country and its industrial capacity. Actually, McNamara spoke of two hundred to four hundred. It is this two hundred figure that President Carter used in 1977 when he asked Defense Secretary Brown to look into the possibility of the United States' reducing its nuclear force to two hundred to four hundred megatons, all carried in submarines.

War of Many H-Bombs.

In 1959 a Congressional Committee held hearings on the effects of a war of many H-bombs. They spent a week on testimony about what would happen if two hundred sixty-three H-bombs with a total of fourteen hundred forty-six megatons of explosive force hit targets in the United States. That would be less than one-tenth of our present stockpile megatonnage. The result was calculated to be fifty million dead and twenty million seriously wounded.

Senator Robert F. Kennedy put it more clearly. In a Senate speech, June 23, 1965, he said: "Eighty million Americans and hundreds of millions of other people would die within the first 24 hours of a full-scale nuclear exchange . . . the survivors would envy the dead." He was repeating what President John F. Kennedy had said in his 1961 speech before the United Nations.

A United Nations Task Force report agrees with their estimate:

> It can be calculated that a hypothetical attack of 10,000 megatons in ground bursts, could, in the course of 60 days, destroy 80% of the population of the United States unprotected, while an attack of 20,000 megatons could cover the entire country with radioactive fallout, killing 95% of the unprotected population.[10]

The massiveness of the destruction cannot be grasped merely by statistics of the dead and wounded. The disaster would be so great that the spirit of humankind would be paralyzed into coma.

What would it be like when the whole country of two great nations was destroyed as viable societies? Those who might survive would certainly judge that the destruction was not worth the result. One thing seems certain to me: nothing we recognize as our free institutions would survive. This is the reason the literature of nuclear destruction has the recurrent theme, "the survivors will envy the dead."

New Weapons Systems.

Despite our overkill capacity and the enormous destructive capacity of our weapons, we are developing new systems with accuracy that shows that we are moving away from our M.A.D. (mutual assured destruction) policy to a first strike policy.

We would not need extra-precise weapons if we were only responding to a nuclear attack. In that case the enemy weapons would no longer be in their silos to be hit.

Weapons less accurate than those we have would suffice for retaliation. The development of more weapons accuracy shows that our policy has changed. Former President Carter expressed this change in his presidential directive 59. What is the message of this presidential directive? The United States will target enemy weapons. That means that we are prepared to strike first. The collateral damage will include the murder of millions of innocent people.

Jimmy Carter was expressing publicly what had already been said secretly.

All our presidents, from Harry Truman to Richard Nixon, have secretly threatened first use of nuclear weapons. If you want to read more about the evidence behind this deeply unsettling information, see the fourth page of Daniel Ellsburg's article, "Nuclear Armaments."[11]

We say that our new policy of targeting enemy weapons is more humane than targeting cities. But, what is the truth of this situation? Neither policy is humane. Consider this—there is no sign that we will not hit both cities and weapons. Besides, many of the weapons targets are near cities. We do not need hard-target-killing missiles unless we are trying to fight and win a nuclear war by initiating a pre-emptive disabling strike on Soviet forces. There are very few hard targets other than missiles that the accuracy of our new missile systems could be directed at.[12]

Our leadership has consistently emphasized that we seek only a nuclear force capable of deterring our opponents. Yet, first strike capabilities are weighed, and we find that what really matters is how the other side views our intentions.

The United States public is being mistakenly led to believe that the continued expansion and increased accuracy of our nuclear forces improve deterrence. In fact, it contributes to Soviet insecurity about the safety and effectiveness of their own nuclear forces. The policy does just the opposite of what we intend. It endangers us more, rather than protect us:

> No first strike by the U.S. or the Soviets can prevent the other side from mounting a massive retaliatory nuclear attack against the aggressor. The Soviets already have more than 7,000 in their strategic long range land, sea and air forces. On the average, each one of these weapons has about 60 times the power of the Hiroshima and Nagasaki bombs. It is estimated that they will have nearly 9,000 strategic weapons by 1985. Even if we were to execute a completely successful first attack, we would still expect three to five thousand weapons to survive for delivery on targets in the U.S. Repeated studies show that such an attack would result in more than 100 million U.S. casualties. Why build a first strike system, if you are unwilling to commit national suicide?[13]

Trident Subs

These huge underwater boats are almost the size of two football fields put end to end—five hundred sixty feet. They move underwater at forty miles per hour. Twenty-four launchers, with seventeen warheads on each launcher, give each submarine four hundred eight warheads apiece.[14]

Each of these four hundred eight warheads is five times the size of the Hiroshima bomb. Their reach is four thousand miles. These deadly underwater boats can kill millions four thousand miles away from the submarine that fires the target. The one that pushes the button that releases this destruction is removed by all these miles from the suffering and agony, the death and the murder that will be performed in the name of freedom, and other wordy concepts.

From the bottom of the sea, two thousand miles off the coast of an adversary, it can destroy targets that are two thousand miles inland.

The total warheads of each submarine give it a total destructive power of fifteen to twenty megatons. Compare that with all the United States bombs dropped on Europe and Japan during World War II. That total was two megatons in explosive power. The cost of these dinosaur destructive mechanisms is two and one half billion dollars each. Twelve are on order, and twenty more are planned.

MX Missile

MX means missile experimental. These missiles are land based, and each missile carries ten warheads with a range of seven thousand miles. Their accuracy is much greater than the Minute Man missiles that are now targeted on Russia. The MX was originally planned to be placed on movable carriers to run on oval shaped race tracks in Nevada and Utah. Now it is planned to replace one hundred Titan and Minute Man missiles in underground silos.

Cruise Missiles

Cruise missiles are drone or pilotless airplanes, launched from under the sea, from the land, or from a plane. The range is about fifteen hundred miles. The cruise missile is very accurate and is able to hit within two hundred feet of its target, with a nuclear bomb ten times the size of the Hiroshima bomb. A special feature is a computerized contour guidance system that allows the missile to fly fifty feet above the ground in such a way that it rises and falls with the land contour and stays underneath the view of radar beams. Its jet engine propels it at five hundred miles per hour.

President Reagan wants to put five hundred seventy-two Cruise and Pershing II missiles in Europe. That would mean that the Pershings (fifteen times the size of the Hiroshima bomb) would be only four minutes away from targets in Russia. His program to increase nuclear armaments in Europe has created extremely strong resistance among the European people. Four million people marched in 1981, protests that were held in major cities all over Europe and England. These protests included Rumania, a so-called Iron Curtain country.

Reagan's missile programs will add seventeen thousand new missiles to our arsenal over the next five years.

After-effects of Nuclear War.

We can make a few calculations about what the after-effects would be, although many of them are beyond our imagination. The massiveness of the destruction would leave medical problems unsolved and insoluble; the absence of water, food, and housing would make the struggle to recover a nightmare; the disruption of the social and economic structure of society might be total. We would be confronted with many entirely new situations, and radiation effects would have given us entirely new selves to try to deal with them. We would not know how to deal with the situations, and we would not know how to deal with ourselves. I have already talked about the possibility of total changes in the ecological systems of plants, insects, and animals, that we must have in order to survive. Soil erosion would be another problem with dimensions of magnitude that we have not known before.

Any situation from everyday life that we can imagine would be entirely changed. Consider a truck driver in an unblasted area. The driver would be worried about contamination levels, and wonder about the safety of going where he needed to go. He would be worried about his family. He would be fearful of another nuclear attack.

He would face psychological and social difficulties that have never been faced before. Would he become like the people who survived the Hiroshima blast, who could only stand dazed and paralyzed by it all and wonder whether it was worth trying again?

This is but a simple summary of how the power of the atom and the development of technology have changed war. No longer is it what it used to be: something man could experiment with, but not be hurt by all that much. The word war no longer means what it used to mean. National suicide would be a better word than war for nuclear conflict. But, many of us still hold the outmoded belief that war can still be survived. We deny the reality that confronts us, and the denial serves to sicken our spirits and confuse our lives.

What morality and love have never accomplished, the end of wars, may now be forced on us by technology. To know the basic destructive power of nuclear weapons is a first step toward peace. It is with knowledge of that destructive power and the defenselessness of any nation against it that President John F. Kennedy put before the world the alternatives that face us: "Together we shall save our planet or together we shall perish in its flames."

A knowledge of the destructive power of nuclear weapons alone would confirm the truth of these statements. That is the reason everyone should be informed about the atomic arsenal and the doom that it holds for all of us.

It is important to remember that nuclear weapons are but a part of our arsenal. We also possess a huge quantity of so-called conventional weapons, and chemical and biological weapons.

The Nuclear Future.

Now, we have looked at the gospel of peace and nuclear technology. They go in opposite directions. They show us how far our practice is from our theory. Yet, they also give us a similar message, "We must cooperate as brothers, or perish as fools." The gospel speaks to us with the strength of faith. If we have no faith, technology tells us, "cooperate or die."

How does "justice" come into this? Justice is an aspect of peace. Peace is the establishment of a just order: "A firm determination to respect other men and peoples and their dignity, as well as the studied practice of brotherhood, are absolutely necessary for the establishment of peace."[15]

The documents of Vatican II here suggest that the war problem is related to almost all other social problems—the under-developed nations, the decaying cities, schools, medical care and many other related problems. So long as we have to spend such vast sums on weaponry, public funds remain unavailable for urgent human needs. Pope Paul VI expanded the role of the peacemaker who must get at the roots of war. Thus, he coined a new word for peace—*development:*

> Extreme disparity between nations in economic, social and educational levels provokes jealousy and discord, often putting peace in jeopardy. As we told the Council Fathers on Our return from the United Nations: "We have to devote our attention to the situation of those nations still striving to advance. What we mean, to put it in clearer words, is that our charity toward the poor, of whom there are countless numbers in the world, has to become more solicitous, more effective, more generous."

> When we fight poverty and oppose the unfair conditions of the present, we are not just promoting human well-being, we are also furthering man's spiritual and moral development, and hence we are benefiting the whole human race. For peace is not simply the absence of warfare, based on a precarious balance of power; it is fashioned by efforts directed day after day toward the establishment of the ordered universe willed by God, with a more perfect form of justice among men.

> Nations are the architects of their own development, and they must bear the burden of this work; but they cannot accomplish it if they live in isolation from others. Regional mutual aid agreements among the poorer nations, broader-based programs of support for these nations, to coordinate these activities—these are the road signs that point the way to national development and world peace.[16]

Justice may be more clearly seen as related to peace if you consider that civil rights, women's rights, worker rights, human rights will all disappear if we have nuclear war.

I define peace with St. Paul, "Jesus is our peace, reconciling both of us (Jew and Gentile) to God in one body through his cross (Eph 2:11-20). Paul defines peace as a three way relationship of reconciliation among myself, my God, and my human neighbor. Not just myself and God! Not just myself and my neighbor, but all three simultaneously—God, myself and my neighbor.

By this definition peace is what simultaneously brings me to union with God and my neighbor—marriage, friendship, church, community. Peace is built on trust and leads to new life, eternal life.

War is just the opposite. It is what separates me either from God or my neighbor: racism, extreme nationalism, oppression of the poor, killing. It feeds on fear, hate and leads to death, even eternal death.

Every work of justice is also a work of peace.

Yet, without nuclear peace, all other works of peace (justice) will suffer. The tap root of violence (and injustice) in our society is our intent to use nuclear weapons. Until we have frontally faced this issue, there is no hope of any large scale improvement of public morality.

One clear evidence of this is that the expense for weapons takes the money from the poor.

President Reagan's projected five year budget of 1.6 trillion for the military amounts to $876 million a day or $608,500 per minute!

World-wide arms cost $550 billion per year.[17] This equals the income of half the world's people. It shows the way justice relates to peace.

In pre-nuclear days there might be some possibility of funding war and human needs. The nuclear age has changed that. Peace is now necessary before we will have funds for the poor.

I do not say much about justice separate from peace because I see it as part of it. I see the top priority in peace making as our intent to use nuclear weapons. Until we put aside that intent, we will have neither the mind nor the money for justice. If we do not bring our nuclear technology into line with our faith, we will lose both our lives and our faith. We can not keep doing what is contradictory to our faith and still keep our faith. The nuclear age is helping to make this clear. This is the reason so many Catholic bishops, like Archbishop Raymond Hunthausen of Seattle and Bishop Leroy Matthiesen of Amarillo, Texas, are speaking out. This is the reason the United States Catholic Conference is preparing a pastoral letter on peacemaking in the nuclear age. Not only are our lives in danger, but our faith is also.

If the nuclear weapons of the communists hit us, they can destroy only our bodies; but, if we intend to destroy millions of communists with our nuclear weapons, we destroy our souls.

NOTES

[1] Quoted in G.H.C. Macgregor, *The New Testament Basis of Pacifism* (Nyack, New York: Fellowship Publications, 1971), p. 98.

[2] Young India, 26 Dec., 1924.

[3] Norman Cousins, *In Place of Folly* (New York: Washington Square Press, 1964), p. 14.

[4] Harrison Brown and James Real, *Community of Fear* (Santa Barbara: Center for the Study of Democratic Institutions, 1967), p. 15.

[5] Thomas Stonier, *Nuclear Disaster* (New York: Pax Publications, 1963), p. 77.

[6] *Ibid.,* p. 22.

[7] Philip Berrigan, *A Punishment for Peace* (New York: Macmillan, 1969), p. 129.

[8] *Washington Post,* 2 February 1968.

[9] *Defense Monitor,* Vol. X, Number 8 (Washington, D.C.: Center for Defense Information, 1982), p. 1.

[10] "The Nuclear Time Bomb: Report to the UN Secretary," *Saturday Review,* Dec. 9, 1967, p. 19.

[11] Conservation Press, Box 201, 2526 Shattuck St., Berkeley, CA 94704.

[12] Robert Aldridge, *Counterforce Syndrome* (Washington, D.C.: Institute of Policy Studies, 1981), p. 7.

[13] "MX: The Weapon Nobody Wants," in *Defense Monitor,* Vol. X, #6

(Washington, D.C.: Center for Defense Information, 1981), p. 4.

[14] Aldridge, *op. cit.,* p. 35.

[15] "The Church Today," in *The Documents of Vatican II,* ed. Walter M. Abbott, S.J. (New York: America Press, 1966), p. 290.

[16] Paul VI, "On the Development of Peoples," art. 76, 77.

[17] Ruth L. Sivard, *World Military and Social Expenditures* (Leesburg, Va.: World Priorities, 1981), p. 5.

Liturgy/ Eucharist/ World

Julia Upton

"The world is too much with us," cried William Wordsworth, against the oppressive pre-industrialized London society of 1806:

> The world is too much with us; late and soon,
> Getting and spending, we lay waste our powers:
> Little we see in Nature that is ours;
> We have given our hearts away, a sordid boon!
> This Sea bares her bosom to the moon;
> The winds that will be howling at all hours,
> And are up-gathered now like sleeping flowers;
> For this, for everything, we are out of tune;
> It moves us not.—Great God! I'd rather be
> A Pagan suckled in a creed outworn;
> So might I, standing on this pleasant lea,
> Have glimpses that would make me less forlorn;
> Have sight of Proteus rising from the sea;
> Or hear old Triton blow his wreathèd horn.[1]

Is the world too much with us? Well, the world certainly is with us. In March we journeyed with Captains Loumas and Stafford aboard Columbia on their Skylab mission, sympathized with their being afflicted with "space tummy," watched excitedly as their moths mated, and kept anxious vigil as a dust storm delayed their return. Twice this past year the world's attention was fixed within minutes as the wires burned with news of imminent tragedy, once on Washington with the attempted assassination of President Reagan; later on Rome, in almost instant-replay fashion, with a would-be assassin's attack on Pope John Paul II. Within minutes—seconds, even—the world—the universe, in fact—is in our living room.

Is the world too much with us? How many nameless brothers and sisters were slaughtered on the streets in El Salvador, Honduras or Guatamala this week? Where are the other thousands who have disappeared this past year? Do we really have a grasp of the magnitude of the political oppression that the people of Latin America are suffering? What is the truth? Whom do we believe? How can the world be too much with us when these answers elude us?

In our technological twentieth-century society, historians say, we have advanced farther scientifically than all previous civilization taken as a whole. Macaulay, Carlyle, and other nineteenth-century social critics drew our attention to the fact that industrialization had caused progress (and population along with it) to increase geometrically rather than arithmetically as it had done in the past. In this atomic age, civilization seems to be advancing exponentially. Technology, population, and their consequent economic problems seem to have gone completely off the charts.

Nothing, save peace, seems to be beyond our grasp. "Mission Control" can take us anywhere we want to go. Last year, Saturn was our destination as we travelled aboard Voyager II, and now we are speeding our way to Uranus, where our estimated time of arrival is January 24, 1986. Outer space, which was our science-fiction world twenty-five years ago, is now our backyard. Given time, surely we can do anything. That is what our lived experience seems to be saying to us.

But, there is another voice speaking to us—a doomsday voice announcing that our technology is out of control. We now possess the technology to obliterate all civilization within a matter of minutes. No one seems to be working hard enough to prevent this ultimate holocaust. An atmosphere of fatalism has begun to pervade the "land of the free and the home of the brave," evident particularly among the young. Children do not think that they are going to grow up. Many people expect that the world will be ripped apart by a nuclear war in this generation or the next.[2] So, fatalism leads to hedonism.

The real world, created by God—the world for which Wordsworth hungered, is too little with us, and so we have manufactured an artificial world where materialism triumphs over humanism and progress becomes our god. "Technology," writes Waldo Beach, "has not only changed the face of the earth; it has changed the human heart."[3] And thus we pray to a new trinity:

> Glory be to the Father, Science, and to the Son, Technology, and to the Holy Spirit of Efficiency, which, although it was not in the beginning, surely is now, and ever shall be, world without end. Amen.[4]

Yes, the world is too little with us, so the world is too much with us. We are trapped in a life-threatening maze, for ours is the Age of Paradox.

Where Did It All Begin?

It was so natural, for we seemed to have all of the answers. The rules of the game used to be that the side with the biggest army, the most guns, and the best plan would win. Now, in the middle of the game, someone has changed the rules. All of a sudden, winning means los-ing—losing everything. The danger is too imminent, the odds too close, and our only hope seems to be to disarm and to put our trust in the God who saves us. Yes, we have the answer, but no one is rushing to be first to act on that answer.

We live in a world of time and space bound by limits, but until now the human race has perceived limits as barriers to be overcome. Testing the limits of everything around us, especially the limits of human endurance, humanity pushes onward. But, there are limits—real lim-its—beyond which one cannot go.[5] We cannot survive a nuclear holo-caust, and we cannot replace natural resources once they are gone. We who were trained to think linearly must begin to think holistically, for we have now begun to mortgage the future.

At our present rate of usage, the world has enough silver to last for twenty years, natural gas for thirty-five years, lead for fifteen years, and mercury for thirteen years.[6] Once they are gone, they are gone, so our present way of living is already sealing the fate of the future. Most frightening of all is the horror we are leaving future generations in the very refuse of today. Radioactive plutonium, for example, a by-prod-uct of the nuclear energy we so blithely discuss as "clean and effi-cient," has a half-life in excess of twenty-four thousand years. The damage that will cause we have only begun to examine. Yes, once again we have the answer, but changing our lifestyle is inconvenient, and we probably do not really believe that "America the Beautiful" could run out of anything, or that our technology will not find a way for danger-ous radioactive substances to self-destruct politely and harmlessly.

There must be another answer—a more comfortable answer. It will just take time, and time will answer everything. In time we will find cures for cancers, just as we found them for polio a generation ago. We work hard to conquer disease. Or do we? Two-thirds of the deaths in the world today are from hunger or from problems related to hunger.[7] Malnutrition affects sixty percent of the population of developing countries.[8] It is quite clear that we know what to do about hunger, as does any child, but still we do not do anything, and in some countries, particularly in Central America, first-world greed and complacency actually put people into a position of forced starvation.

Does the liturgy have any relation to this world marred by fatalism and hedonism, to this world on the brink of nuclear obliteration, where we are rapidly depleting natural resources while seventy million people are on the brink of starvation? Many of those who are focusing their attention on social justice issues both from an ecclesial and a global perspective do not think that the liturgy addresses those issues, and often claim that instead liturgy numbs people to the importance of those issues. Beyond the critique of social activists, however, the liturgy, when properly understood, can "speak to the weary a word that will rouse them" (Is 50:4).

The Role of the Liturgy

The key phrase is "properly understood." When liturgy is seen as a pompous display of ecclesial wealth and power, it is not liturgy. When we talk about attending or hearing mass, we are not discussing liturgy. When we conclude that the obligation to attend the eucharistic liturgy refers only to our physical presence, we have failed to understand what liturgy is all about. As Rafael Avila writes, "When Eucharist fails to exert any significance in the life of the Church, and when Christians feel estranged by the sacrament, something is seriously amiss."[9] Yes, something is seriously amiss—we do not know what liturgy is and what it can be for the People of God, and so for this, too, "we are out of tune; it moves us not." We must rediscover the wonder that is liturgy.

The word "liturgy" is Greek in origin. Its root, λειτουργία, literally meant "service for the sake of others." So, any service performed for others—serving in the army or caring for the destitute—would have been considered as liturgy. Extant sources, however, use the word only in a religious context, so liturgy has come to connote only religious service for the sake of others, or more properly, public worship.[10]

The well-hidden secret, however, is the concept that public worship is actually service for others. From a ministerial perspective it seems to be logical enough, but how can one member of the congregation actually be serving the rest of the congregation? That seems to be the root of our present-day difficulties with understanding that liturgy, most especially the Eucharist, is the "source and summit of our life as Christians."[11] In the past liturgy has been seen as something that is done for us—having Father say Mass for us. Thus, the worshipping community was placed in a position of relative passivity precisely when it was being called, in Eucharist, to be most authentically active. Eucharist is *the* celebration of who the Christian people are:

> For it is through the liturgy, especially the divine Eucharistic Sacrifice, that "the work of our redemption is exercised." The liturgy is thus the outstanding means by which the faithful can express in their lives, and manifest to others, the mystery of Christ and the real nature of the true Church.[12]

This failure to understand the true nature of the liturgy is an age-old problem, and stems from two different roots. In one respect we have been plagued with the disease of minimalism, even in our "ex opere operato" sacramental theology, for centuries. The rich young man has been our model:

> And there was a man who came to Jesus and asked, "Master, what good deed must I do to possess eternal life?"
> Jesus said to him, "Why do you ask me about what is good? There is one alone who is good. But if you wish to enter into life, keep the commandments . . . ."
> The young man said to him, "I have kept all these. What more do I need to do?"
> Jesus said, "If you wish to be perfect, go and sell what you own and give the money to the poor, and you will have treasure in heaven; then come and follow me."
> But when the young man heard these words he went away sad, for he was a man of great wealth (Mt 19:16-18, 20-22).

Nine first Fridays, five first Saturdays, slipping into Mass for the three principal parts, getting the Office in by mumbling Lauds at 11 p.m., we were mired in the spirituality of "getting by." Were we so different from our relic-hungry, indulgence-hoarding ancestors? Salvation was a privatized affair. We had travelled far from the dinner table that night in the Upper Room.

Another root of our problems of misunderstanding the liturgy lies in the very architecture of our churches—an architecture that speaks a body language of passivity. From intimate gatherings of the faithful in house churches in the first three centuries, by the twelfth century the altar—the common table—had moved to a back wall, and another wall had grown up physically separating the community from the celebration. To this day we suffer from that distant alienation, and neither ritual reform nor architectural renovations have completely overcome its effects.

In order to counteract these effects and to understand how liturgy can actually be service for the sake of others and compel us to be the followers of Jesus we name ourselves, we must begin even farther back than the Upper Room. First, it is necessary to examine the place and significance of ritual itself in the human community.

Ritual in the Human Community

Ritual, cutting across all times and cultures, is rooted in the common experience of humanity, anthropologists tell us.[13] Human beings have a predeliction for ritualizing the significant events of their lives. Births, deaths, passages to adulthood and to new states in life are all events that call us to attention, so we pause and savour the significance of the moment. Using words, symbols, and actions, we highlight an event to such an extent that we engrave it deeply on our memories and thereby make it available for us to re-experience periodically. In a communal context ritual is a social drama which embodies the experiences of the community. By repeating the pattern of symbolic actions that are the ritual, we evoke the feelings of the primordial event that called the particular community into being.[14]

There are several characteristics of ritual, from the anthropological perspective, that, when present, enable the participants to benefit from the experience:[15]

a. By drawing our attention to a limited stimulus field, the ritual sharpens our focus.

b. The words, symbols, and actions expand the optic and allow us to savour the significance of the moment.

c. The presence of others is both supportive and festive.

d. At the same time, other life circumstances seem to fall away for the moment, allowing the ritual to be a flow experience that both relaxes and strengthens the participants.

If we take the birthday ritual as a case in point, we can see how these characteristics are operative:

a. Our attention is focused on the person being feted.

b. How this particular optic is enlarged depends almost exclusively on the relationship we have to the person. A mother would probably recall the birth itself along with other significant birthday rituals. Whatever the relationship, however, we are drawn to reflect on the importance of that person in our life.

c. The presence of others is of significance because their experience of the guest of honor expands everyone else's experience.

d. Relaxation, enjoyment, refreshment and nourishment, furthermore, are the by-products of the autotelic nature of ritual.

The quality and intensity of the ritual are not insignificant, nor are they determined by the elaborateness of the ritual. Rather, the quality and intensity, shown by the hearts of the participants, consequently determine the value of the ritual. Poor quality and lack of intensity in ritual celebration will hinder sharpening the focus or expanding the optic, and will empty the ritual of its meaning. That was the thrust of the Old Testament rebuke:

> "What are your endless sacrifices to me?"
> says Yahweh.
> "I am sick of holocausts of rams
> and the fat of calves.
> The blood of bulls and of goats revolts me.
> When you come to present yourselves before me,
> who asked you to trample over my courts?
> Bring me your worthless offerings no more;
> the smoke of them fills me with disgust.
> New Moons, sabbaths, assemblies—
> I cannot endure festival and solemnity.

Your new Moons and your pilgrimages
I hate with all my soul.
They lie heavy on me,
I am tired of bearing them.
When you stretch out your hands
I turn my eyes away.
You may multiply your prayers,
I shall not listen.
Your hands are covered with blood,
wash, make yourselves clean" (Is 1:11-17).

It was not an empty ritual the Lord Jesus longed to celebrate with his friends. At the time it might have seemed rather confusing and ominous for the Apostles, but, in retrospect, it was the ritual that actually made sense out of all those terrible events they experienced in Jerusalem the following days. Truly they came to know Jesus in the breaking of the bread.

Eucharist in Early Christianity

Because the first Christians expected an imminent Second Coming, they did not build a lasting kingdom here, or even document their temporary kingdom. Therefore, our historical data base with regard to the liturgy is meager at best. Taken collectively, however, the data do lead us to make certain assumptions with regard to the celebration of the Eucharist.[16]

A persecuted people, the first Christians gathered in their homes to celebrate Eucharist—to remember Jesus, his message, and his mission. It was the Eucharist and the community gathered in celebration that strengthened and sustained them in those terrible days of persecution. This was their collective remembering of what it meant to have one's body broken and blood shed for another. Eucharist was the center of their life.[17]

Their ritual was simple, the *Didache* records:

> Now about the Eucharist: This is how to give thanks: First in connection with the cup:
> "We thank you, our Father, for the holy vine of David, your child, which you have revealed through Jesus, your child. To you be glory forever."
> Then in connection with the piece (broken off the loaf):
> "We thank you, our Father, for the life and knowledge which you have revealed through Jesus, your child. To you be glory forever.
> "As this piece (of bread) was scattered over the hills and then was brought together and made one, so let your Church be brought together from the ends of the earth into your kingdom. For yours is the glory and the power through Jesus Christ forever."[18]

At the conclusion of their meal, they prayed in thanksgiving for the meal shared, for the Church, and for the coming of the kingdom:

"Let Grace come and let this world pass away.
"Hosannah to the God of David!
"If anyone is holy, let him come. If not, let him repent.
"Maranatha!
"Amen!"[19]

Always their plea, "Maranatha!" They were a people of faith. They believed deeply in the Lord Jesus, trusted that he would return, and worked at the risk of their very lives to live the way Jesus lived until his return. There was, therefore, an important social dimension to their celebration of the Eucharist. They brought offerings for "orphans and widows, and those who were in want on account of sickness or any other cause, and those who were in bonds, and the strangers who were sojourners among them, and . . . all those in need."[20] From the celebration, furthermore, they went to bring the Eucharist to the sick and the infirm, showing us that this sharing was an integral rather than secondary element of their eucharistic feast.

Outlawed, persecuted, hunted down, these Christian ancestors of ours were making a political statement in their Eucharists. Ronald Marstin writes:

Wherever faith is bent on building the truly reconciled (as distinct from merely pacified) society, the Eucharists will be divisive, exposing the discrepancies between the Gospel we profess and the oppression we tolerate, and pressing us to align ourselves either with those who would change the system or those who would resist the change.[21]

So spoke the Lord, Jesus: "Do you suppose that I am here to bring peace on earth? No, I tell you, but rather division" (Lk 12:51). So, the first Christians lived and died.

Eucharist and the Christianization of the World

A turning point came in 313 A.D. with Constantine's Edict of Milan tolerating Christianity. By the end of the century, when Christianity had become the official religion of the Roman Empire, Church and state were wedded in what would prove to be one of the most unhealthy and unfortunate matches in all of civilization. Gradually, Christianity began to take on the dress, customs and classist mind of the state.

Eucharists became more and more elaborate and stylized; churches began to spring up in towns and villages, and the poor and needy began to be neglected. Bishops like Basil the Great, Theodore of Mopsuestia, and John Chrysostom cried out against such abuse:

> Do you wish to honor the Body of Christ? Do not despise him when he is naked. Do not honor him here in the church building with silks, only to neglect him outside, when he is suffering from cold and nakedness. For he who said, "This is my Body" is the same who said, "You saw me, a hungry man, and you did not give me to eat." Of what use is it to load the table of Christ? Feed the hungry and then come and decorate the table. You are making a golden chalice and you do not give a cup of cold water? The Temple of your afflicted brother's body is more precious than this Temple (the church). The body of Christ becomes for you an altar. It is more holy than the altar of stone on which you celebrate the holy sacrifice. You are able to contemplate this altar everywhere, in the street and in the open squares.[22]

But their cries fell on deaf ears, and the attitudes they condemned are with us still.

The conflict of which this speaks, ironically, can actually be a catalyst for uniting and strengthening Christian communities today, for it is just such conflict that forces us to renew our commitment to Christian values of justice and mercy, rather than to the cultural values of upward mobility and maximization of profit.[23] The Christian worldview sees a basic interpenetration of the members of the human community, which opposes the hierarchical world-view that inexorably leads to injustice and oppression. "It is mercy I want, not sacrifice" (Hos 6:6). It is mercy, then, that is fundamental to our eucharistic meal. With compassion we celebrate with quality and intensity, quite unlike the spirituality of "getting by." Such a ritual is anything but empty, and truly we participate in the service of each other.

Eucharistic Spirituality

Because Eucharist celebrates the Church's identity, it can never be a private reality. God became human, not to be worshipped, but to serve and to teach us to serve. In *Bread Broken and Shared* Paul Bernier points out that the New Testament accounts of the Eucharist should be read in that light. They were not written to teach us about Eucharist, but to develop further truth. Thus, Bernier writes, the Eucharist is "our extension of the Incarnation, and it gives us a focal point toward which everything can and should relate."[24]

When we look to the New Testament we see, first of all, in the synoptic accounts the evangelists' attempts to clarify the meaning of Jesus' suffering and death. From them we draw the words of consecration, but those words go beyond being yet another sacramental formula, for they give us the true meaning of that meal, the significance of Jesus' life, and the meaning of his death. The accounts are not identical, as we can see by placing them side by side.

In chapter 14 of Mark's Gospel we read:

> . . . as they were eating he took some bread, and when he had said the
> blessing he broke it and gave it to them. "Take it," he said, "this is my
> body." Then he took a cup, and when he had returned thanks he gave it
> to them, and all drank from it, and he said to them, "This is my blood,
> the blood of the covenant, which is to be poured out for many. I tell you
> solemnly, I shall not drink any more wine until the day I drink new wine
> in the kingdom of God (Mk 14:22-25).

Matthew's account differs only slightly in two further expansions.
Whereas Mark's account says that the blood of the covenant "is to be
poured out for many," Matthew's account says that it is "to be poured
out for many for the forgiveness of sins" (Mt 26:28), filling out the
understanding of the meal itself and the events which followed. The
closing line of the Last Supper account also differs slightly in Matthew,
whose sentence reads, "I shall not drink wine until the day I drink the
new wine *with you* in the kingdom of my Father" (Mt 26:29).

Luke's account of the Last Supper refers to the kingdom of God as
well, but does so twice and in a slightly different style. He writes, "I
have longed to eat this passover with you before I suffer; because, I tell
you, I shall not eat it again until it is fulfilled in the kingdom of God"
(Lk 22:15-16), and he goes on to cite the Lord saying, "I shall not drink
wine until the kingdom of God comes." Luke's account is also the only
one that calls for the apostles to repeat this action: "This is my body
which will be given for you; do this as a memorial of me" (Lk 22:19).

We find one more account of the Last Supper in Saint Paul's first
letter to the community of Corinth. Here Paul goes beyond the event of
the Last Supper to a more developed interpretation of its significance:[25]

> For this is what I received from the Lord, and in turn passed on to
> you: that on the same night that he was betrayed, the Lord Jesus took
> some bread, and thanked God for it and broke it, and he said, "This is
> my body, which is for you; do this as a memorial of me." Until the Lord
> comes, therefore, every time you eat this bread and drink this cup, you
> are proclaiming his death, and so anyone who eats the bread or drinks
> the cup of the Lord unworthily will be behaving unworthily toward the
> body and blood of the Lord (1 Co 11:23-27).

Apparently the people of the community came together for the meal,
and behaved very greedily, and so Paul chastised them for not being
aware of what they were about in celebrating the Eucharist.

There is no literal description of the institution of the Eucharist at
the Last Supper in the Johannine corpus. This silence, rather than
being seen as an omission or lacuna in the development of a eucharistic
spirituality, is actually rich in meaning, for the Johannine allusions to

Eucharist and his description of what transpired at the Last Supper have greatly enhanced our spirituality.

In the sixth chapter of John's Gospel we find what is known as the "Bread of Life" discourse, and this is considered to be the core of John's teaching on the Eucharist. Here Jesus compares himself with manna—the food of the covenant with which Yahweh-God fed the Israelites as they wandered in the desert. Besides being the food of fidelity, the manna was also food for the faithful, and was not allowed to be hoarded. This is what we see as the foundation of John's interpretation of Eucharist.

The foot-washing sequence which appears later in John's Gospel is thought to have taken place during the Last Supper. Rather than including an account of the institution of the Eucharist, John includes this act of love and service by Jesus. This substitution is of significance, for by so doing John unites Eucharist to the creation and support of the human community through service.

Therefore, we see that the New Testament accounts of the institution of the Eucharist evidence a development of understanding related to the events that took place in the Upper Room the night before Jesus died. Only in the light of the Lord's death and resurrection did that meal come to take on full significance, and did so as an outgrowth of the Lord Jesus' entire ministry among us on earth.

Eucharistic Themes

An understanding of what liturgy and ritual are intended to be, an examination of the development of the eucharistic liturgy, and a reflection on New Testament eucharistic spirituality lead to identifying certain eucharistic themes:

    a. Eucharist as meal;
    b. Eucharist as presence;
    c. Eucharist as memorial;
    d. Eucharist as renewal of the covenant;
    e. Eucharist as call.

As is true with Avery Dulles' models of the Church, these themes are not mutually exclusive. Each is a necessary component of the liturgical theology of the Eucharist, and each nourishes and supports the others. Each of these themes helps us to expand our understanding and experience of sharing and being Eucharist, while taken together they encompass the whole thrust of Christian life.

Eucharist as Meal

There is something fundamentally human about sharing a meal. We rarely come together that we do not eat. Our guests are barely in the door before we ask, "May I get you something to drink? Would you

like something to eat?'' Although we do not often reflect on the significance of those familiar words, this ritual has two dimensions. First, we
are responding to hunger, and second, we are sharing ourselves and
our resources. Distinctions are erased, barriers are lowered, injuries
are healed, and enemies are reconciled as people gather together to
break bread.

While the Last Supper was surely the most significant meal Jesus
shared with his friends, it certainly was not the only meal recorded in
Scripture. Understanding these meals helps us to see more clearly how
Jesus used the occasion of a meal. We find a whole ''meal ministry,'' in
fact, that enables us to deepen our understanding of Eucharist.[26] We
know, for example, that Jesus taught and forgave at meals, often
breaking bread with people whose reputations were less than respect-
able in the society of that day. The table sharing of Jesus, therefore, is
yet another reflection of his preaching of the reign of God, where the
barriers between God and sinners would be destroyed. ''The reality
symbolized by the Eucharist,'' writes Michael Crosby, ''is to be normative for the Church's life. All people are equal because all share in
the one meal as tablemates.''[27]

If you can recall your most profound experience of being hungry,
you will remember how it qualifies one's whole consciousness. Nothing else matters, food becomes an obsession, and assuaging that hunger becomes the main thrust of one's activity. Its pain gnaws away deep
inside, sapping one's energy and deadening one to the rest of life.
Hunger, in varying degrees, to be sure, is a global experience. Beyond
this brutalizing characteristic, however, hunger is also a constant
reminder of our basic dependency. We are not totally self-sufficient,
but rather dependent on others for the food we need to stave off
starvation.[28]

Jesus calls himself the ''bread of life,'' and as his followers we are
called to be ''bread'' for others. There is a flawed belief abroad in our
land that only people with an adequate food supply can fully appreciate
Eucharist. I am not so sure that the opposite is not rather the truer
statement. Although we might not all be hungering for food, our
hoarding ways indicate that we are hungering for something—security, for example. Physical hunger, then, has analogues in the other
hungers of the world, and being ''bread'' for others is not any more
limited to feeding the hungry than the Lord's being bread was. It
commands us to nourish others by our very lives.

In coming to the eucharistic meal we testify to our common belief
that it is the Lord Jesus who sustains and nourishes us, and pledge that
we will likewise sustain and nourish one another with the bread that is
our lives. That is our pledge to humanity. In his address to the Forty-
first International Eucharistic Congress in Philadelphia, Father Pedro
Arrupe reminded us that ''if there is hunger anywhere in the world,
then our celebration of the Eucharist is somehow incomplete

everywhere in the world."[29] The move toward completing our celebration of the Eucharist, therefore, necessitates addressing the issue of world hunger in a concrete way.

Eucharist as Presence

Eucharist is also an immersion in the mystery of presence. For almost two thousand years now Jesus has been present to those who believe as they gather in his memory. True, there have been myriad explanations for this phenomenon—theologies galore—but, while some scholars grapple with finding the intellectual construct capable of expressing the inexpressible, the people of faith have been grasped by the mystery—lured into the passion of presence.

"I will be with you all days, even to the end of the world," Jesus promised. We trust the promise because we have known love, and it is love that leads us to plumb the mystery of presence. When I was five years old, my mother took my sister and me to visit my grandmother. I remember being heartbroken at the thought of leaving my father here in New York as we traveled to this place called South Dakota. Dad took me for a walk one evening before we left, and looking up at the moon he said, "Julie, just go outside at night and look up at the moon. We'll be looking at the same moon, and we'll be together." That was one of the best lessons I have ever learned—a lesson about love, about presence, about God.

Jesus promised to be with us, but we control the quality of presence. There are times when I am so scrunched on a subway train that for survival's sake I must close my eyes and actually shut myself off from the experience of that crushing presence at hand. A quiet walk on the beach is so much more enjoyable, so I close my eyes and wander off. Just as I can, at times, choose to wall myself off from the mystery of presence, I can also manage to heighten my awareness of it, by allowing myself to be captivated by its allure. Our theologizing about the mystery of real presence in the Eucharist has often been sadly incomplete. Once again, caught in the trap of minimalism, we have been duped into thinking that real presence is simply a definition or a doctrine and not primarily an experience.

Mysteries engage us, and for that very reason "mystery" is a marvelous word for God and for Eucharist. A mystery begins with an experience: a sudden noise in the middle of the night; a fleeting glimpse of a shadow that startles us; an unexpected voice that calls us in the middle of the night. "What was that?," we respond in reflex, and are lured into the mystery. Grasping at clues, and trying to fit them together, we might end with a definition, but to relate only the solution is to negate the thrill of mystery. How dull to read only the endings of Agatha Christie mysteries!

Beginning and ending with the doctrine, however, are only part of
this limitation, because the mystery of presence in the Eucharist actually goes beyond the presence of Jesus—another dimension of the
mystery upon which we rarely reflect. The ritual itself leads us beyond
the presence of Jesus and enhances the quality of presence because
ritual time is a journey into the καίροσ. That unity of timelessness
allows one experience to build on another, and to deepen the phenomenon of presence. There, in that time-beyond-time, we join our tablemates—the community of the baptized of yesterday, today and tomor-
row, gathered from all the corners of the earth. The words of the third
eucharistic anaphora remind us:

> From age to age you gather a people to yourself,
> so that from east to west
> a perfect offering may be made
> to the glory of your name.

Eucharist as Memorial

It is inescapable that Eucharist also memorializes the passion and
death of the Lord Jesus, for it is in Eucharist that the sacrifice of the
cross receives its meaning. "Viewed theologically, the passion of Jesus
was the consequence of his fidelity to his Father and his fellow human
beings," writes Leonardo Boff.[30] As a memorial, then, Eucharist is
also an uncomfortable reminder to us of where the consequences of our
fidelity might lead. When Jesus finished the Last Supper, he said, "Let
us go to the Garden of Olives," and we know where that path led.
Where do we go?

John Westerhoff relates the story of meeting an escaped political
prisoner in Paraguay, who described an Easter celebration in the
prison two days before. While non-Christian prisoners kept the guards
occupied, the Christians huddled together. Their pastor, a fellow prisoner, began:

> "This meal in which we are part, reminds us of the prison, the
> torture, the death, and the final victory and resurrection of Jesus Christ.
> He asked us to remember him by repeating this action in the spirit of
> fellowship. The bread which we do not have today, but which is present
> in the spirit of Jesus Christ, is the body which he gave for human ity. The
> fact that we have none represents very well the lack of bread and the
> hunger of so many millions of human beings. When Christ distributed it
> among his disciples and when he fed the people he revealed the will of
> God that we should all have bread. The wine which we do not have
> today is his blood present in the light of our faith. Christ poured it out for
> us to move us toward freedom, in the long march of justice. God made
> all persons of one blood: The blood of Christ represents our dream of a
> unified humanity, of a just society without difference of race or class."

The pastor told of a man, about sixty, whose daughter had died fighting with the guerrillas, who commented, "I think this communion means that our dead are alive, that they have given their bodies and blood making Christ's sacrifice their own. I believe in the resurrection of the dead and feel their presence among us." There was silence and the pastor continued, "This communion is not only a communion between us here, but a communion with all our brothers and sisters in the church or outside, not only those who are alive, but those who have already died. But still more it is a communion with those who will come after us and who will be faithful to Jesus Christ." He then told us how he held out his empty hands to each person placing his hand over theirs as they together boldly exclaimed, "Take, eat, this is my body which is given for you; do this in remembrance of me. Take, drink, this is the blood of Christ which was shed to seal the new covenant of God with humanity. Let us give thanks, sure that Christ is here with us, strengthening us." Then they raised their hands to their mouths and received the body and blood of Christ and after sharing the kiss of peace returned to their life in prison with new hope.[31]

Eucharist as Renewal

The words Jesus used at the Last Supper renewed the covenant—God's promise to be with us through time, now in the presence and memory of God incarnate. It called to mind another meal—a meal of promise[32]—celebrating another time when Yahweh-God intervened in history to redeem and liberate an oppressed people. The liberation which God wrought for God's people was a political revolution—a violent political revolution. It prefigured the subsequent liberation of the whole of humankind in Christ. Yahweh-God has been faithful to the covenant, which reached its ultimate expression in the death and resurrection of the Lord Jesus. It did not, however, end there, for it continues being renewed again and again as Christians gather together in the Lord's name.

"Giving oneself" ($\delta o \upsilon \lambda o \acute{\upsilon} \epsilon \iota \nu$) involves liturgical overtones, for it is both a style of life and a liturgical expression that are connected to total submission to another.[33] Breaking the eucharistic bread and distributing it is not only recognizing that Christ's gift is meant for everyone, but it is also joining personally in the play of giving. "To participate in the Eucharist," writes André Fossion, "is to be invited to make the same journey; not only to exchange goods and words, but also to bring our very life into the system of giving."[34]

It was that dimension of the life of the Church that the Fathers of the Second Vatican Council were attempting to address in their renewal of the liturgy:

> No Christian community . . . can be built up unless it has its basis
> and center in the celebration of the most Holy Eucharist. Here,

therefore, all education in the spirit of community must originate. If this celebration is to be sincere and thorough, it must lead to various works of charity and mutual help, as well as to missionary activity and to different forms of Christian witness.[35]

The call for "radical" changes in the liturgy, therefore, did not stem from a diminished devotion to Jesus, but rather from a deeper understanding of the nature of the priesthood of Jesus which by baptism we promise to continue.[36]

In comparing the liturgical life of the Church of today with that of previous centuries, Tissa Balasuriya recognizes that in the past liturgy was geared toward personal salvation in an individualistic sense, building up the Church, and consequently glorifying God, while today the needs differ. Today's needs are for:

a. Personal fulfillment with freedom and responsibility.

b. The realization of the values of justice, truth, freedom, love, equality and peace within human societies.

c. The building of a just world order and a new society.

d. Communion with cultures, religions and ideologies that are not of Christian inspiration.

e. The growth of the Christian communion in the service of the human person.[37]

Renewing our covenant as expressed in the Eucharist today, therefore, requires also a new approach to ecclesial life: deep personal and interpersonal reflection, new theological accents, socio-political analysis and options, action and evaluation, forming of alliances, risk-bearing, new lifestyles, new modes of being a Christian community, and a spirituality of the person and of the human community.[38]

In his book, *The Spirituality of the Beatitudes,* Michael Crosby illustrates the cycle into which this places the Christian community. First, one has an experience that jars the worldview that has previously guided one's life. This leads one to call into question the very ideology that at another time undergirded one's understanding of existence—the world and God. Rejecting this former concept of God, therefore, one returns to the source—to Scripture—in search of similar experiences others might have had. Here, one finds a new understanding of God, who is now revealed as part of this new experience of the world, part of one's life and part of the life of the world.[39] This is the cycle we have seen operative in the liturgical life of the Post-Vatican II Church.

Eucharist as Call

Finally, as meal, presence, memorial and renewal, Eucharist is also ultimately a call—a call for Christians to serve and to celebrate. This is not a reality which can be effected overnight, we have found. Ritual renewal is part of the process, as is architectural re-design, but at root is the. desperate need for conversion. Looking back to the New Testament, we see that for Jesus the Eucharist was fundamentally action-oriented. Balasuriya describes it as a "fundamental option to die rather than to live with compromise," for Jesus trusted in the survival of his message, not his body.[40] Celebrating Eucharist and bringing about the reign of God, it follows, demand that we experience that same confidence in God's presence that we may be continually converted to God's authority.

κοινωνία, therefore, is the greatest need of the Church today, for it is that spirit of community that compels us to serve and to celebrate in and through the Eucharist. We have seen that in the early Church the community was not a gathering of the "already converted," but the place where people lay themselves open to genuine conversion.[41] Father Arrupe sees, consequently, that our eucharistic commitment is calling us to a new form of solidarity.

Eucharistic Solidarity

> In the Eucharist we receive Christ hungering in the world. He comes to us, not alone, but with the poor, the oppressed, the starving of the earth. Through him, they are looking to us for help, for justice, for love expressed in action. Therefore, we cannot properly receive the Bread of Life unless at the same time we give bread for life to those in need wherever and whoever they may be.[42]

When the Lord Jesus took the bread into his loving hands, blessing, breaking and sharing it, he was concretely demonstrating for us the proper use of all material goods. It was this way of life that the early Christians followed, eucharistizing their lives by blessing God in all things and allowing others to share in their possessions. The simplest eucharistic celebration, therefore, reviles against injustice at any level in our society, particularly when we turn goods entrusted to our care into weapons that wield power and destruction.[43]

It is important to understand the prophets' critique of empty rituals as a basis for comprehending what is still lacking in contemporary rituals. Their criticism consisted of three fundamental ideas:

a. Ritual was not connected to history and was celebrated as a rite simply "floating" in history without either reflection on or questioning of it.

b. It coexisted passively with injustice.

c. It appeared to possess a magical character.[44]

Once, then, the ritual—particularly the Eucharist, which should be the center of Christian living—loses its meaning, Christianity itself becomes irrelevant. Balasuriya sees this happening in a domino-fashion:

> When Eucharist ceases to relate to integral human liberation it ceases to be connected with Christ's life sacrifice; it does not then build human

community; it does not, therefore, help constitute the kingdom of God on earth; it does not even honor God objectively.[45]

The logical conclusion, then, would be to return to the world, for it is of primary importance that a reconciliation be effected between liturgy and contemporary society. The religious person, we have come to know, is the truly human person; the religious celebration, it would follow, is the truly human celebration. This was the way that the Latin American bishops, gathered together at the Medellin conference in 1968, approached the liturgy. "The liturgical celebration," they wrote, "crowns and nourishes a commitment to the human situation, to development and human promotion."[46] For them liturgy was viewed as a "stop along the way"—a place where community would festively celebrate its history as well as its paschal, eschatological meaning.[47]

Over the centuries, what has happened has been a gradual decline of common meaning.[48] The death and resurrection of the Lord Jesus is the paradigmatic event for the Christian community. The early Church, we saw, endeavored to preserve and to prolong that event within the community by means of signs, symbols, sacred texts, music and dance, forming a ritual. Prolonging, savouring the event that gave them identity as a people was the natural expression of the Christian community. They were compelled to celebrate—obligated by identity rather than by law. That is the point to which the Christian community must return. If the Eucharist is once again seen as *the* event of the Christian people, as the remembering necessary to continue the ministry of Jesus, as the celebration of active, continuous concern for others, the peripheral changes commonly associated with liturgical renewal will not engender so much consternation. The interior change will be so overwhelming and so obvious that externals will be of little consequence. Such a liturgical celebration would contribute precisely what the bishops at Medellin called for:

    a. A more profound knowledge and living experience of the faith.

    b. A sense of the transcendence of the human vocation.

    c. A strengthening of the spirit of community.

    d. A Christian message of joy and hope.

    e. The missionary dimension of the life of the Church.

    f. The demand presented by faith to commitment to the human situation.[49]

Mercy: Foundation for Life and Liturgy

"It is mercy I desire, not sacrifice" (Hos 6:6). Those words echo again and again in scripture, in the life of the Church, and in the lives of the followers of Jesus. It is mercy, therefore, that must permeate both the law and the cult. All of our sacrifices, whether they are liturgical rituals or the daily ministry of our lives, should express Yahweh-God's mercy to those in need. Without such compassion, our sacrifices will be devoid of Yahweh-God, and our ecclesial structures will be barren vestiges that give tribute to human folly.[50] "Compassion," writes Matthew Fox, "operates at the same level as celebration because what is of most moment in compassion is not feelings of pity but feelings of togetherness."[51]

That quality of mercy must be the foundation for a truly human community if we are to survive into the next millennium. Mercy, that flowed with every word and action of the Lord Jesus, must once again be the bedrock of ecclesial life, not the new code of canon law or the latest apostolic exhortation. These are not unimportant, but they are not the identifying element of the Christian community.

Conclusion

We have returned to where we began—with the lived Christianity of the world of 1982. Ours is a world moving at supersonic speed, racing madly nowhere. The truly human person, the truly Christian person, is an alien living in a foreign land, and rather than being divorced from this condition, the liturgy, especially the Eucharist, is intimately bound up with contemporary life. We need the liturgy to nourish us, to sustain us, and even to liberate us. Although that might seem to be an impossibility when so many so-called liturgical celebrations are not liturgy at all, but rather pompous displays of hierarchical structure and power. We can not leave it there, however, and blithely conclude that the liturgy does not speak to our world. Instead, we must believe that it is possible, and dream it into reality.

NOTES
[1] *The Mentor Book of Major British Poets,* ed. Oscar Williams (New York: The New American Library, 1963), p. 68.
[2] Jim Wallis, *A Call to Conversion* (San Francisco: Harper and Row, 1981), pp. 72-109.
[3] Waldo Beach, *The Wheel and the Cross: A Christian Response to the Technological Revolution* (Atlanta: John Knox Press, 1979), p. 11.
[4] *Ibid.,* p. 15.
[5] Elizabeth and David Dodson Gray and William F. Martin, *Growth and Its Implications for the Future* (Branford, CT: The Dinosaur Press, 1975), p. 65.
[6] *Ibid.,* p. 75.
[7] Wallis, p. 70.
[8] Gray, p. 72.
[9] Rafael Avila, *Worship and Politics* (Maryknoll: Orbis, 1981), p. 2.
[10] Often in the post-Vatican II era the word "liturgy" is mistakenly limited to reference to the Eucharist. The eucharistic liturgy is but one of our liturgical celebrations, which include all of the sacraments and the liturgy of the hours as well.

[11] *Constitution on the Sacred Liturgy [CSL]*, no. 10, in *The Documents of Vatican II*, ed. Walter M. Abbott, S.J. (New York: America Press, 1966), p. 142. All further references to conciliar documents are to this text.

[12] *CSL*, no. 2, p. 137.

[13] Cf. Mircea Eliade, *Patterns in Comparative Religion* (New York: Sheed and Ward, 1958); Victor Turner, "Passages, Margins and Poverty: Religious Symbols of Communitas," *Worship* 46 (1972): 390-412.

[14] John H. Westerhoff, "Contemporary Spirituality: Revelation, Myth and Ritual," in *Aesthetic Dimensions in Religious Education,* ed. Gloria Durka and Joanmarie Smith (New York: Paulist, 1979), p. 24.

[15] Victor Turner, "Ritual, Tribal and Catholic," *Worship* 50 (1976): 504-26.

[16] Cf. Josef A. Jungmann, *The Early Liturgy* (Notre Dame: University of Notre Dame Press, 1959).

[17] Avila, p. xii.

[18] *Didache* 9, in *Early Christian Fathers [ECF]*, ed. Cyric C. Richardson (New York: Macmillan, 1970), p. 175.

[19] *Didache* 10, pp. 175-76.

[20] Justin, *First Apology* 67, *ECF,* p. 287.

[21] Ronald Marstin, *Beyond Our Tribal Gods: The Maturing Faith* (Maryknoll: Orbis, 1979), p. 45.

[22] Tissa Balasuriya, *The Eucharist and Human Liberation* (Maryknoll: Orbis, 1979), pp. 26-27.

[23] Cf. Regis Duffy, "Unreasonable Expectations," *Proceedings of the Catholic Theological Society of America* 34 (1979): 1-17.

[24] Paul Bernier, *Bread Broken and Shared: Broadening Our Vision of the Eucharist* (Notre Dame: Ave Maria Press), pp. 11-40.

[25] Monika Hellwig, *The Eucharist and the Human Hunger of the World* (New York: Paulist, 1976), pp. 13-17.

[26] Bernier, p. 27.

[27] Michael Crosby, O.F.M.Cap., *Spirituality of the Beatitudes: Matthew's Challenge for First-World Christians* (Maryknoll: Orbis, 1981), p. 154.

[28] Hellwig, pp. 13-17.

[29] Pedro Arrupe, "The Hunger for Bread . . . ," *Address to the 41st International Eucharistic Congress,* Philadelphia, 1976.

[30] Leonardo Boff, *Way of the Cross—Way of Justice* (Maryknoll: Orbis, 1980), p. ix.

[31] Westerhoff, p. 25.

[32] Although the last meal Jesus ate with his friends may literally have been a celebration of the Passover, Scripture scholars are not in agreement on the point. Figuratively, however, the connection is inescapable.

[33] Crosby, p. 61.

[34] André Fossion, "The Eucharist as an Act of Exchange," *Lumen* 35 (1980), p. 416.

[35] *Decree on the Ministry and Life of Priests*, no. 6, pp. 545-46.

[36] Balasuriya, p. 118.

[37] *Ibid.,* p. 133.

[38] *Ibid.*

[39] Crosby, p. 15.

[40] Balasuriya, p. 17.

[41] Wallis, p. 109.

[42] Arrupe, *op. cit.*

[43] Mark Searle, "Serving the Lord with Justice," in *Liturgy and Social Justice,* ed. Mark Searle (Collegeville: Liturgical Press, 1980), p. 28.

[44] Avila, p. 27.

[45] Balasuriya, p. 38.

[46] Medellin, "Liturgy," no. 4, in *CELAM: The Church in the Present-Day*

Transformation of Latin America in the Light of the Council, vol. 1 (Washington, D.C.: Latin American Bureau, USCC, 1968), p. 132.

[47] Avila, p. 76.

[48] Cf. Edward K. Braxton, *The Wisdom Community* (New York: Paulist Press, 1980).

[49] Medellin, no. 6, pp. 132-33.

[50] Crosby, p. 146.

[51] Matthew Fox, *A Spirituality Named Compassion* (Minneapolis: Winston Press, 1979), p. 4.

Spirituality and Justice: An Evolving Vision of the Great Commandment

William R. Callahan, S.J.

Oscar Romero had always been a pious man. A solitary, exact person, he easily flowed into the Roman routine of study at the Gregorian University. When he went back to El Salvador, he was a natural choice to be the general secretary of the Bishops' Conference, where he gave years of cautious, faithful service.

In February 1977, Monsignor Romero was appointed Archbishop of San Salvador. The landowners, political leaders, the military and traditional church circles were delighted to have someone they knew and trusted. They knew that Romero would rein in the so-called "subversive" church people, those priests and religious who had begun to work with communities of the poor.

Among those who knew him well, Romero was judged a pious, conservative, "churchy" priest, who loved liturgical rules and clerical discipline. His appointment as archbishop brought apprehension to the church people who worked with the poor in the cities and countryside. Their only consolation was that he was reputed an honest and prayerful man, and that his health was reported to be fragile.

Within a month of his appointment, the National Guard massacred two hundred to three hundred people in Plaza Libertad where they were demonstrating against the recent fraudulent elections. Father

137

Rutilio Grande, the first Jesuit priest to live and work with the poor, was assassinated near Aguilares.

A cruel persecution was launched against church people who worked among the poor and against the native faith leaders, who were emerging in these communities. "Delegates of the Word," local people who took responsibility for coordinating activities of the "communidades de base," became frequent targets of assassination.

Romero, who had stayed largely uninvolved in the struggles of El Salvador, began to talk to the people and listened to the stories of the survivors at Plaza Libertad. He went to the death site of Rutilio Grande, and from those experiences began his final three year pilgrimage. He began to "accompany the poor on their journey." He began a ministry so like that of Christ that it would lead to his assassination.

The journey would take Romero along paths that never before had he walked. His relationships to people and to institutions differed sharply from his previous life.

Previously, Romero had been a bishop who made decisions by himself. He now began to consult widely.

Previously, he had tried to avoid too close identification with any group. He now began to commit the church to the poor.

Previously, he had been circumspect, handling church affairs with great caution. Now, through his pastoral letters and radio broadcasts, he became a powerful public voice speaking on behalf of the poor of El Salvador.

Previously, he had spoken vaguely of the nation and its problems, urging personal conversion. He now began to speak concretely, describing both the suffering of the people and the sources of that suffering, the unjust system, the powerful oligarchy that perpetuated the injustice, and the violence and terrorism with which they struck back at any people who sought change.

Romero's path was not an easy one. He denounced the violence of both the popular forces and the security forces. He struggled with his own doubts and his heritage of remaining aloof. At times, divisions came between him and some of his collaborators over the choice of means to be used to support the people. At the same time, save for his friend Bishop Rivera y Damas, he faced a painful split between himself and the other bishops.

As the church, under Romero, began to accompany the people, it came under fierce persecution. Several priests were assassinated and others exiled. Romero's radio station was repeatedly bombed. Death threats began to multiply against his own life.

Romero refused personal protection, even after the uproar which took place in February 1980, when he appealed to President Carter to cut off economic and military aid to El Salvador.

"Your government's contribution, instead of favoring the cause of justice and peace in El Salvador, will surely increase injustice here and

sharpen the repression against the people's organizations fighting to
defend their most fundamental human rights.''

Romero would die on March 24, 1980, while offering the Eucharist,
with an assassin's bullet in his heart. Evidence strongly suggests that
the killer was hired in a plot headed by Major Robert D'Aubuisson,
recently elected head of the Salvadoran Assembly.

Although largely ignored by Rome, which has delayed for more
than two years in appointing a permanent successor, Monsignor
Romero is already being venerated as a saint by the ordinary people of
Latin America. They celebrate his life as that of a person who followed
Jesus, walked the same road with the poor and died, as Jesus did, a
violent death on their behalf.

THE GREAT COMMANDMENT: SPIRITUALITY AND PRAYER

The closing years of Monsignor Romero's life illustrate the powerful developments taking place in spirituality and ministry as Christians
respond to the church's call to nourish faith by building justice in the
world.

I would like to reflect briefly on the heritage of our spirituality and
then articulate developments which are taking place in our vision of life
in the great commandment. After outlining some dimensions of a
healthy spirituality which can support such a vision, I will apply the
reflections to the life of Monsignor Romero.

Specifically, I would like to treat the following:

1. Where people of faith have a choice, the priorities of their prayer
and ministry, and the spirituality that flows from these, are deeply
affected by their vision of life in the great commandment.

2. The monastic vision emphasized that our relationship to God
should be primary in our lives. This vision powerfully dominated
Catholic thinking on prayer and spirituality so that it became the
primary model for Christian prayer and spirituality.

3. A new vision of life in the great commandment is emerging in
Catholic thought and practice, a four-fold vision. This vision celebrates relationships not only to God but to near and distant neighbors.
It stresses commitment to the work of justice as a central dimension of
life in the Gospel.

4. This vision of Christian living demands a major expansion of our
spirituality, including the development of prayer which can flourish in
the midst of active, even conflictual, lives. Such conflicts inevitably
surround efforts to bring forth greater justice upon the earth.

5. These developments in prayer and spirituality appear resonant
with the life and praying of Jesus.

6. There are several marks of a healthy Gospel spirituality which
can flourish in the midst of active living. It should be: built upon

experience: simple: deep and loving: tough and durable: socially conscious: hospitable.

7. The final ministry of Monsignor Romero provides a place to test the development of such spirituality.

THE HERITAGE OF FAITH

1. *Where people of faith have a choice, the priorities of their prayer and ministry, and the spirituality which flows from these, are deeply affected by their vision of life in the great commandment.*

Jesus summed up his dreams for us in the great commandment. We are called to love God "with all your heart, with all your soul, and with all your mind, and with all your strength . . . Love your neighbor as you love yourself" (Mk. 12:30-1).

This general vision statement of following Jesus has stirred Christian hearts throughout the ages. It is not detailed but leaves to the believer the means by which this vision will be lived out.

For many Christians throughout the ages, the very poverty of their existence dictates most of the choices of their lives. Their option is to struggle for survival.

But in all lives, even the most poor, the vision we take of the great commandment colors the very thinking by which we view our lives.

The great commandment gives a perspective by which to weigh reality and to make judgments. That it is a call to love, is clear. From then on, the choices are left up to the followers of Jesus to interpret according to their particular time, place, culture and position within their culture.

Christians throughout the ages have tried to build ways of living which articulated this commandment for their age. In different eras, a focus on a particular way of fulfilling the great commandment has led to differing understandings of Christian life and service.

Jesus, when questioned, "And who is my neighbor?" (Lk. 10:29), had replied with the beautiful parable of the Good Samaritan.

The Early Church

Early Christians sought to live this two-fold love of God and neighbor in the spirit they remembered from Jesus. Building upon the Jewish life and culture from which they came, they gathered to celebrate the Eucharist, extended a loving welcome toward one another and welcomed in new members who heard the preaching, believed in Jesus and wished to join this Jewish community of Jesus' followers.

The style of prayer and ministry was Jewish until persecutions and the wide-ranging ministry of some of the disciples brought new converts from other cultures.

The advent of these converts posed great challenges for the way in which "neighbor" was understood. In the early years, "neighbor" meant Jewish people, just as Jesus had generally restricted his ministry to Jewish people.

In the great struggle described in Acts, the community, after much pain and struggle, finally broke forth from its Jewishness to affirm that people could become followers of Jesus and keep their own cultural identity.

When the original expectations of Jesus' swift return to earth slowly faded, the community began to develop its own institutional patterns, priorities, theology and lifestyle.

While the persecutions were frequent, they often served to knit the community about survival needs. But, when Christianity was accepted by Rome, lay people soon fled to the desert both in reaction against the change and in a deeper search for God.

2. *The monastic vision emphasized that our relationship to God should be primary in our lives.*

The monastic vision of the great commandment proclaimed the primacy of love for God above all things, a powerful emphasis upon the first part of the great commandment.

This vision did not deny love of neighbor; it simply focused upon the direct encounter with God and all that aided this dynamic.

Begun by lay people who fled to the desert alone and then gradually aggregated in communities, the monasteries were institutions where the members sought to give glory to God in various spiritual exercises which help us to find God: recitation of the Office, vocal prayers, Eucharistic celebrations, private prayer, spiritual reading, reflection upon the Scriptures, listening to religious instruction, et cetera.

These exercises were soon arranged into an ordered pattern, the "order of the day," a regular rhythm of prayer and work surrounded by an ambience of silence and tranquility which encouraged that inner serenity which helped the person meet God.

Human experiences which introduced "noise" were controlled or eliminated. Monasteries sought isolation on hilltops, cliffs, or in remote areas. Contact with families, friends, or any visitors was sharply limited.

Within the community, everything sought to foster an atmosphere of silence conducive to prayer. The rules of silence, the grand silence from evening until morning, the strict silence during the days, encouraged the person to seek and live with God.

The experiences which produced "inner noise" were controlled by renouncing these experiences, the way of negation and mortification for the sake of greater freedom.

Concern for spouse, children, family, companionships, et cetera was controlled by celibacy, with further inner controls on sexuality through garb, separation and group living. Worry over possessions, money, taxes, et cetera was controlled by the vow of poverty. Concern for a job, decision-making, and other life-choices were limited by obedience which, through the "order of the day" and the guidelines for religious life proper to particular communities, provided constant guidance for particular decision-making. Frequent rotation of tasks encouraged a person not to become "attached" to some particular job.

Interpersonal relationships were restricted through the structures of community life which limited visitors and kept contact among community members under strong control.

Contact with the larger society in which the monastery existed was kept minimal. Only a few people were authorized to interact with the outside world.

The entire lifestyle of the monastery or convent was arranged to encourage the members of the community to keep their hearts focused on their primary relationship to God.

The Impact on Christian Spirituality

The monasteries became centers of learning and culture, remaining so during the so-called "Dark Ages," when Europe was in turmoil. Monastic writers and teachers spoke enthusiastically of their experiences of God and of the lifestyle which made such prayer and living possible.

For societies in turmoil and conflict, the vision of serenity and tranquility was like a breath from heaven. In addition, no comparable developments took place in popular piety, where the Eucharistic liturgy grew silent, unintelligible and remote, leaving the people in a limbo between devotion and superstition.

Thus, the powerful example and enthusiastic communication from the monasteries controlled Christian expectations of deep prayer from the fifth century onward, impacting on the spirituality of the later, active communities, and the life of ordinary Christians.

Active Communities

When active religious communities arose, especially during the time of the Reformation, the inner life of the communities carried with them the monastic expectations of prayer. This put strong tension between the active ministry and the life of silence and apartness. Active ministry was still viewed as dangerous, although necessary. Only regular withdrawal for prayer and religious experience could avoid the peril of becoming an "activist."

Fervent houses of active religious sought the ambience and even the routine of the monasteries. Houses of formation sought the rural isolation typical of earlier monasteries, thus setting up expectations of life and prayer which would affect religious from active communities and channel their expectations of praying.

Ordinary People in the Church

The monastic experience and writings conditioned Catholics to believe that there is a special class of praying people called "contemplatives" who were the specialists in prayer. They did the deep praying for the church and lived the lifestyle which supported that "higher way," the "way of the counsels," the "way of perfection."

Lay people who lived the less demanding "way of the commandments," who lived caught up in the "cares of the world," obviously could not aspire to the "lofty" prayer of the monasteries since they could not (would not) take on the demanding lifestyle needed to achieve such prayer.

These people prayed in ordinary ways, i.e., vocal prayer, going to mass, saying the Rosary, and other pious practices which could help them with their important, but modest, faith task of living the commandments.

These people still had a chance for a high place in heaven since God judges us according to our generosity in responding to the graces given us. Thus, even though not called to the heights of prayer and love for God expected in the convents and monasteries, lay people might love God with proportionately greater generosity and thus win a higher place in heaven.

For lay people whose good will and lifestyle permitted it, some approaches to prayer were adapted from the religious orders. Retreat experiences, regular mental prayer and other religious exercises sought to carry over some of the benefits of prayer, silence, serenity and detachment.

THE GREAT COMMANDMENT: A NEW VISION

3. *A New vision of life in the great commandment is emerging in Catholic thought and practice, a fourfold vision.*

The growth of urban living and the impact of modern thinking, especially in psychology, sociology, science and theology, brought a vast expansion of emphasis upon the personal and interpersonal dimensions of Catholic thought.

The Second Vatican Council welcomed much of this thinking. The Council, reinforcing the early social call of Pope John XXIII, sounded a theme that has been reaffirmed repeatedly, i.e., a call that Christians are to follow Jesus by involving themselves in the struggle to begin God's reign here upon the earth, a community where people try to love one another and to extend that love throughout society in the work of justice.

Effects of the Changes

Vatican II and the currents it recognized have had a profound impact upon Christian life. Biblical renewal, a revitalized interest in directed retreats, houses of prayer, the cursillo movement, charismatic renewal, and fresh understanding of the Eucharist have emerged.

Especially striking has been the effort to build personal union with Christ in prayer, a direction which has encouraged new openness to interpersonal love as the basis of our living.

However, the conviction that we are not merely to love near neighbors, but to love distant neighbors through efforts to transform the unjust social structures of our world—an inherently conflictual process of change—marks a serious challenge to traditional interpretations of prayer and spirituality.

Whereas the encouragement to interpersonal bonding has found general favor, the emphasis upon societal love through the work of justice is more threatening.

The call to action and involvement is perceived as threatening, drawing a person away from prayer and faith, into a dangerous world of temptation, worldly cares and unbelief.

The rapid social changes, the challenges to traditional values, living patterns, religious practice, et cetera could lend support to this view of a breakdown in faith and religious experience.

But, another interpretation is possible, i.e., that we are being summoned to a new vision of life in the great commandment in which involvement in the cares of this earth, far from being a distraction to our primary concern for God, becomes the very core of our journey in following after Jesus.

Such a fundamental shift in our religious vision neccessarily calls forth a shift in images of prayer and religious faith.

The Call to Justice

The Council and the subsequent church social teaching summon us to a vision of the faith community working upon this earth to bring forth the beginnings of the reign of God. This is a task for all the people of God, sharing life and ministry, each in accord with his or her gifts.

The work of salvation is expressed not only in private faith and in interpersonal love with near neighbors, but includes as a constitutive and necessary dimension the effort to reach out and embrace sisters and brothers of the earth with whom we are joined in societal bonds.

Working together, we seek to effect societal transformation that nourishes justice and struggles to overcome both personal sin and that evil which is embedded in the unjust structures of society—social sin.

This work of justice is not on the periphery of faith, but in the central core of life as a Christian, a constitutive dimension of the preaching of the Gospel. Openness to such efforts is integral to healthy Christian faith. Support for such a way of life is integral to a healthy spirituality.

Yet, the work of justice, seeking to transform the unjust structures of society, involving as it does efforts to effect change, is inherently conflictual. To live this way and to grow deeply prayerful take an expansion, not only of our priorities of living the great commandment, but in the way in which we live, pray and follow the demands of this call to love.

This expansion of spirituality does not involve an adaptation of monastic spirituality, but the development of a complementary tradition of prayer and spirituality based upon involvement, a spirituality reflecting a fourfold vision of the great commandment.

The Great Commandment—A Fourfold Vision

The great commandment can now be described as an interplay among four major dimensions: our direct love and relationship to God, our relationships to near neighbors with whom we can form interpersonal bonds, our relationship to ourselves which is the foundation on which we build love for our neighbors, and our societal relationships to distant neighbors.

Just as Einstein's four dimensional approach to the universe, which added time as a fourth dimension to the three dimensions of space, demanded an expansion of our vision of the physical universe, so also this four dimensional approach to life in the great commandment demands an expansion in our vision of Christian living and of our expectations of prayer. Such an expansion seems possible, necessary and fruitful.

This fourfold approach to the great commandment is a fourfold approach to the way that God comes to us and in the way that we draw near God. The experience of God and God's love comes through each dimension of Christian living. Our expectation of prayer must expand to integrate these experiences.

4. *This vision of Christian living requires a major expansion of our spirituality, including the development of prayer which can flourish in the midst of active, even conflictual, lives.*

A major transition in our spirituality is to nurture a supportive mindset which celebrates human activity upon the earth and makes such insertion, our following of Jesus, the substance of our faith and prayer.

In such a vision, we work out our salvation by following after Jesus in a life whose words and activities attempt to express, each in our own unique way and aggregated together in various communities, the spirit of Jesus.

All dimensions of this living of the great commandment can become an expression of our faith, hope and love. All dimensions of this living become different facets of the experience of God. All dimensions of this living can form the substance of our praying, and prayer becomes a crucial dynamic for integrating each dimension of life in the great commandment.

Thus, we bond with God directly in prayer, whether its focus be Jesus, God our Father and Mother, or the Spirit of God.

But, prayer can also bond us with our near neighbors, people who have names and faces, with whom we can form personal ties. It can build ties with distant neighbors for whom prayer must be our primary vehicle for bonding, commitment and solidarity. Prayer can become a way of loving and accepting ourselves in that truthful, contemplative gaze that helps us experience ourselves in a way analogous to the way God experiences us, thereby strengthening us to take responsibility for our lives.

This embrace of the earth is what God did in becoming a human being and, in so doing, recommended human existence as a beloved way of life. Jesus became one with us, shared our existence and our struggles, including our struggle with evil and with death. Through Christ's embrace of our earth salvation came to all of us. We work out our share in and responsibility for that saving love by following after Jesus in a life whose decisions, actions and relationships celebrate faith, hope and love.

Prayer of Insertion: Praying Life

Prayer has been described as "the raising of the mind and heart to God." An expanded description, in keeping with a fourfold view of God's life coming to us in the great commandment, is "the raising of our minds and hearts to all the dimensions by which we experience God in living the great commandment."

In this vision, the faith experience which flows from any dimension of our life can become an experience of praying, an experience of faith-bonding which integrates our lives and strengthens us for further following of Jesus.

If this be true, then not just times apart from involvement can grow prayerful, but the way is opened for contemplative bonding through-out active, busy lives.

Trained as we are to consider silence and apartness necessary to prayer, especially contemplative prayer, we face a major challenge to break open new categories for prayer and spirituality. Yet, we have the example of Christ to encourage us.

THE EXAMPLE OF JESUS

5. *These developments in prayer and spirituality appear resonant with the life and praying of Jesus.*

Christ took on our human existence in Israel, grew up in Nazareth and engaged in a public ministry that led to his being killed to stifle the threat he was posing to Jewish authorities.

The Scriptures tell of his active ministry, especially among the poor, the marginal people of Israel, to whom he brought Good News of salvation, that they were the beloved people of God.

As people flocked to him seeking relief for their sufferings, the ministry grew demanding and consuming.

Although he sometimes went apart to pray, moments that were special enough for the Scripture writers to comment on them, the bulk of his time was spent with his disciples and the people to whom he ministered, healing the sick, raising the dead, teaching the good news to the poor, liberating people from their sins and welcoming all to the reign of God.

Since he was soon noticed by authorities who first observed him, then tested him, then began a campaign to neutralize and negate him, tensions and conflict soon swirled around the ministry. The threats grew so tangible that when he resolved to respond to the news that Lazarus was dead, Jesus encouraged the disciples to go up and die with him. And indeed, death soon followed.

The Prayer of Jesus

During his ministry, Jesus sometimes went apart to pray. Where the content is described to us, Jesus appears to be praying over the events of his life and ministry. In the desert, he reflected on the direction and style of his ministry, coming forth to minister among the lowly of Israel. He prayed the night before he chose his close disciples. On Tabor, he spoke with Moses and Elijah about the forthcoming events in Jerusalem. In the Garden, he prayed through his paralyzing anxiety and dread at the death he sensed lay directly ahead.

Jesus went apart at other times where the content of his prayer is not described. It is clear that the practice was a recurrent dimension of his ministry. Yet, the practice was exceptional enough for the highly selective Gospel writers to mention it as something special.

Nevertheless, Jesus showed a special bonding with life and with people he met that suggests a powerful dynamic of integration in love, typical of what we hope for from deep prayer.

Some have suggested the Beatific Vision, however controlled, was its source, enabling him to live in the continual presence of God. Others suggest the times of prayer apart nourished him for the active ministry.

Yet, an added possibility is that Jesus prayed throughout his ministry, sometimes going apart for perspective and rest, but largely finding nourishment and prayer in the daily experience of his life and ministry, by contemplating the people and events of life as he encountered them, drawing prayerful nourishment and insight from the very experiences as they took place, i.e., that Jesus lived a contemplative posture toward life and brought this contemplative habit to the people whom he met and to the unfolding of his ministry and personal consciousness.

Unless we wish to follow a model for Jesus' insight caricatured as "looking at the Divine Plan each morning" to find out whom he would meet and how he should act and speak, we are encouraged to ask how Jesus in the midst of a busy, active ministry, surrounded by growing tension and conflict, managed to live in love and solidarity with the people he encountered.

The question is important because Jesus lived an active ministry that is more typical of the noisy, active lives of present day Christians, than it was of Christians during the centuries when most lived as subsistence farmers.

If Jesus was like us in all save sin, then perhaps he used dynamics for prayer and activity that we can follow.

The Contemplative Posture of Jesus

Many events of Jesus' life fall in place if we assume that Jesus approached the experiences of his life with a contemplative "gaze" such that he bonded with people and the experiences of his life while they were taking place.

If Jesus contemplated people as he encountered them, we have some explanation for the way in which he could bond so quickly with the woman who began to wash his feet with her tears during the dinner at the house of Simon the Pharisee.

This would explain how, from the midst of a crowd, Jesus could see the tree-borne Zacchaeus and dare to invite himself to the home of this prominent and despised man for a lunch that would redirect Zacchaeus' life and energies.

If Jesus approached life contemplatively, we have some understanding of how Jesus, confronted by the Canaanite woman who sought healing for her daughter, could put aside his normal, Jewish prejudice toward outsiders that led him first to ignore her, then to speak disparagingly, but finally, under her insistent pressure, to break through and acknowledge her great faith and her claim to his ministry.

Contemplating people as he encountered them would suggest a way to understand how Jesus could see little children so differently from his disciples, and how he could penetrate the brokenness of leprosy, blindness, deafness and deformity that so many brought to him.

An habitual contemplative approach to the earth could explain his simple and luminous use of natural events in his teaching. It could also explain the perspective he brought to the strictures of the law. He generally took guidance from the law, but he did not hesitate to heal a broken person on the sabbath, nor talk alone, publicly by the well, to the often married Samaritan woman.

A contemplative heart and habit could place even the soldiers' action of nailing him to the cross against a perspective of forgiveness, and also enable him to reach across the distances separating the two crosses with a pledge of companionship in paradise for the penitent thief.

A contemplative dynamic can interpret the Scriptures' description of Jesus' prayer and fasting in the desert when he prayed over his future ministry. It can illuminate the way in which Jesus gazed at his fears, his call, and at the love which God bore him in order to integrate and heal the vast dread that seized him in the Garden.

The assumption that Jesus habitually contemplated his life's experiences gives us some coherent way to understand how, if Jesus was like us in all save sin, he could live and love as he did in the midst of a noisy, active, turbulent, conflictual ministry.

The societal scope of his contemplation, which carried such conviction of his mission to the people of Israel, seems obvious in his prayer of frustrated love over Jerusalem: "Jerusalem, Jerusalem, you that kill the prophets and stone those who are sent to you! How often have I longed to gather your children, as a hen gathers her chicks under her wings, and you refused!" (Mt. 23:37).

Following his resurrection, when Jesus appears to his disciples, his contemplative gaze reaches out to the whole world. He sends the apostles forth with the charge: "Go, therefore, make disciples of all the nations: . . . !" (Mt. 28:19).

Summary

Although the sketch is brief, the life of Jesus suggests that it is possible for us who follow Jesus to live and to flourish in the midst of the same type of active, busy life that Jesus lived.

There are signs that Jesus approached life with a contemplative posture that enabled him to bond with people and events, even when the ordinary dynamics of human bonding were not present. Rather than have recourse to explanations which take Jesus away from the need to struggle with the same human experiences which we face, it seems valid to suggest that Jesus brought such an habitual, contemplative posture to his life and ministry that the very experiences brought contemplative bonding and nourishment.

If this be true, then perhaps we might build similar contemplative habits for our own lives, habits of prayer which can enable us to follow Jesus in our busy, active lives, and to flourish as prayerful people in the very midst of such living.

Such contemplative habits might enable us to develop a life of prayer such as that which seems present in Jesus, i.e., sometimes going apart to be alone with God, to gain relief and perspective, but finding the bulk of our prayer and faith nourishment in the contemplative bonding we experience within the ambience of God revealed in the people and events of our daily living.

This praying might be called "noisy contemplation."

MARKS OF A HEALTHY SPIRITUALITY

6. *There are several marks of a healthy Gospel Spirituality which can flourish in the midst of active living.*

Several dimensions or marks seem integral to prayer which can help ordinary people to flourish in the midst of active lives, including lives closely engaged in the struggle for justice.

Such spirituality and prayer should be: a) built upon experience; b) simple; c) deep and loving; d) tough and durable; e) socially conscious and enabling; f) hospitable.

a. *Built upon Experience*

This prayer is for the millions of people who try to live the great commandment and to live with love in their hearts toward God, toward themselves and toward neighbors near and distant.

The basic place where ordinary people must encounter God is in their experiences of life. It is here that God's spirit comes to them and guides them. It was in the experiences of his own life and ministry that Jesus came to understand and "own" his call. The path is no different for each of us, either as individuals, or for us collectively.

Thus, healthy prayer in the great commandment is built upon and welcomes the experiences of our lives. Far from being distractions from praying, these experiences offer the very content for our praying over our relationships to God, to ourselves and to our neighbors.

Just as Mary "pondered" events in her heart, just as Jesus prayed over the events of his life, e.g., prayed in the desert over the style of his forthcoming ministry, prayed over the choice of his disciples on the night before he chose them, spoke on Tabor about his forthcoming suffering and death in Jerusalem, and used prayer in the Garden to integrate his anguished feelings, so we too can make the events of our living the integral base of our praying.

Far from being a vision of prayer as a way to keep our hearts focused
on God and thus undistracted and untempted by the allure of the
world, this vision sees our call as a summons to follow Jesus and so to
live and act that the community of God grows stronger upon the earth.
Prayer becomes a powerful dynamic to integrate human experience
and to encounter God throughout the entire range of our daily existence.

b. *Simple*

If prayer is to be available and possible for the millions of Christians
whom Church teaching summons to use their talents to minister upon
the earth and to live fully the great commandment, then the "lifestyle"
of such spirituality must be so simple that people are not summarily
excluded from even attempting it by their lack of resources. That is,
this prayer must be able to flourish in the very middle of the busy lives
which most Christians are living.

If this simplicity in praying is not possible, then deep prayer over a
life of living justly is ruled out by the lifestyle expectations. For example, if deep prayer can flourish only in a milieu of silence and separation from the cares and anxieties of this world, then most people are
thereby excluded from even thinking about such a life. This has been
the traditional barrier to broadening the number of Christians who
attempt a more deeply prayerful way of life.

If, however, a life of praying deeply can build upon our daily experiences and be so simple that we can begin to build such habits as
children when we learn vocal prayers, and continue to develop these
habits as we grow up, then a person of good will might grow hopeful of
attempting such a way of life.

The living of the great commandment is a call to every follower of
Jesus, not an invitation to a carefully screened élite. Great learning was
not the lot of the early disciples, although people of great learning have
found deep nourishment.

Christ came to call the masses of the people, especially those who are
poor and suffering, for whom the Good News is an ultimate call to
perduring faith, hope and love. Deep prayer, sufficient to support them
in their life's struggles, must be simple enough and accessible enough
to them to acquire it.

Therefore, our expectations of prayer and spirituality for active,
busy people must be grounded in simplicity.

c. *Deep and Loving*

Jesus did not come to call disciples who would commit their lives to
the Good News in a moderate, cautious way. He came to call people to

a total way of living in which deep love and radical commitment to the Gospel were the invitation that he proffered.

The rich young man was pious and observant, a good person. But, he could not accept Jesus' invitation to a total commitment.

Jesus' call to love invited a total opening of our hearts where the only guarantee would be faith. It was an invitation that stepped well beyond the demands of Jewish faith.

No longer could they relish "an eye for an eye, and a tooth for a tooth," as Menachem Begin still quotes approvingly. Jesus calls us to put aside vengeance, be reconciled and even love our enemies, praying for those who persecute us (Mt. 5).

Jesus invited people, not toward a faith that can endure a bit of challenge, but toward a radical faith which cannot long be deterred even by loss of wealth, destruction of our good name, or even by death itself.

He clearly invited Christians to become passionate followers with a love that reaches not only to family and friends who love us in return, but toward people still hostile or to those who can make no response.

To the motley crowd that gathered about him, less than the seeming upper crust of Palestinian society, he preached a proud message. "You are the salt of the earth." "You are the light of the world." "Your light must shine . . ." (Mt. 5:13:14:16).

It is a bold love to which Jesus calls us, even when we, like the disciples, feel timid. He promised that when the time comes, the Spirit will give us words, teaching us everything that he had taught.

The boldness is needed by disciples, for our task, as he told the disciples before he ascended, is to "Go out to the whole world; proclaim the Good News to all creation" (Mk. 16:16).

Thus, any spirituality which adequately reflects the Gospel must support a deep, passionate, committed love for God, for ourselves, and for our sisters and brothers near and distant.

In our new "Age of the Martyrs," when many of the martyrs are created by people who claim Christian faith, our spirituality must support prayer which enables an ordinary person to grow toward a deep, abiding love.

d. *Strong and Durable*

A key test for any spirituality is whether or not it strengthens a person to follow Christ more closely or whether it sets up such expectations of fragility and peril that the person is rendered less capable of vigorous participation in building the reign of God.

Strength and durability are especially key for a Christian vision which accepts concern and action on behalf of justice as a constitutive dimension of living the Gospel.

When Jesus preached, a hallmark of his preaching, and a hallmark of Christians who followed him, was that he raised their sights of power for love that lay within them, promising that His spirit of love would make possible things that they could not conceive.

Jesus constantly challenged them beyond their cultural limits. No longer an eye for an eye or a tooth for a tooth, but a putting aside of revenge. No longer "love your neighbor and hate your enemy," but "love your enemies and pray for those that persecute you" (Mt 5:43-44).

Jesus challenged them to forgive not seven times but seventy times seven, and challenged their emphasis on possessions and security. He encouraged them to trust that God's love for them was more than that borne the sparrows of the air and the lilies of the field.

Jesus challenged them in word, and he challenged them in deed by acting out forgiveness when he was being killed and by forgiving them their cowardice when he rose. He was meek and yet bold before Pilate. He challenged the leaders of the Jewish state for loving honor and riches more than service of God, and he was willing to lay down his life for his friends and the Good News which he came to preach and to be for us.

Jesus gave personal witness of the strength and durability which he pledged to people who believed in him and followed him. That strength and durability are a key sign of a healthy faith.

When the Vatican Council II begins its document, "The Church in the Modern World," it celebrates this strength by embracing the earth and the struggles of God's people.

"The joy and the hopes, the griefs and the anxieties of the people of this earth, especially those who are poor or in any way afflicted, these too are the joy and hopes, the griefs and anxieties of the followers of Christ. Indeed, nothing that is genuinely human fails to raise and echo in their hearts" (*Church in the Modern World,* #1).

In repeated documents over the last twenty years, the church has recounted this embrace of the experience of the people of God in their journey after Jesus.

The journey is a challenge. Our faith and prayer must support such a way of life.

e. *Socially Conscious*

Formerly, the Christian vision could look comfortably upon a faith consciousness that focused only on God: "God above all things."

While this may sometimes be the special call of a few, it is inadequate for most. Nor can we rest any longer with a purely personalist vision of faith, whether its focus be "me and Jesus" or an attempt to restrict our concerns to interpersonal relationships. Interpersonal relationships are good, but they are simply incomplete, just as adolescents with their preoccupation with themselves have not yet matured.

The most powerful, and still emerging, modern development in faith and spirituality is the call to develop a societal consciousness and commitment to support the work of justice, which is now seen, not as on the periphery of faith, but at the core of a healthy, adult faith.

It is precisely in this area of involvement and activity that we should expect the development to be slow and struggling. The concepts imply a substantial redirection of Catholic thought and expectations. Our heritage of many centuries is fearful and hostile to involvement in "the world," seeing it as a powerful source of temptation to faith and destructive of religiosity.

Such a major shift in Christian vision, as noted in the "social gospel" struggles of the Protestant churches, should be a struggle that continues for the foreseeable future. Out of the dialogue should come a new and deeper understanding of Christian faith.

But, some dimensions are already emerging: an expanding sense of the religious call to work for justice; a realization that faith and salvation are not merely individual events, but a collective journey of a community; that social structures deeply control not only behavior, but moral values and feelings as well; that religious faith acted out is inherently political; and that the work of justice, since it involves change of unjust structures, or defense of just ones in the face of efforts to change them, invariably involves tension, conflict and struggle.

Coming as we do from a religious heritage that instinctively viewed conflict, tension and struggle as unhealthy, a disturbance of the peace and tranquillity judged essential to praying, the direction of Christians toward societal involvement stirs trepidation. This suspicion occurs despite the strong witness that Jesus was killed, not for the good he did, but because of the political pressures which his religious ministry put upon the leaders of Israel.

In the changing climate of religious experience, we are only beginning the lengthy process of building a nurturing, enabling spirituality to support Christian living that includes societal love—the work of justice.

f. *Hospitable*

The call of our faith is to embrace the world in love. Our salvation is worked out in companionship and solidarity with others.

A powerful test of healthy spirituality and sound praying is that it encourages the person or community who follows Jesus to an ever deepening hospitality. This has ever been true.

Christ made it clear that God loves all people, a bold proclamation to make in a culture that viewed separatism as essential to national survival.

The struggle to welcome the Gentiles into the early community stirred the deepest conflict. The path of hospitality was the breakthrough that opened the church to the entire world.

The early Benedictine communities, even when they proclaimed stability, offered such open arms of hospitality that their reputation for welcome extended far and wide.

It seems almost a truism that persons who seek to follow the great commandment and to love God, themselves and neighbors near and distant, will act out that love in hospitality toward others.

Yet, it is a recurring temptation of Christians and those of any faith to be exclusive. The conflict of centuries that followed the Protestant Reformation destroyed hospitality among people of divergent beliefs. The loss of hospitality added further religious fuel to the national, racial, ethnic, sexist prejudices that people seem to cherish.

Yet, Christ called us to open our hearts to all. He acted out this welcome especially to the outcasts of his society, those who might least expect such welcome. He told us that it is when we give away our lives that we find them, just as it is only when the grain of wheat falls to the earth and dies that it can bring forth life a hundredfold.

No matter how much Western society has encouraged Christians to "watch out for #1," the central core of Christ's teaching remains true and is witnessed in experience. It is when we open our hearts and give our love away that we find love.

Noisy Contemplation

Although the subject is too large to be dealt with in detail in this essay, a spirituality and approach to prayer do appear to be emerging which offer the possibility of deep prayer for ordinary people, a prayer modeled after the life, ministry and dynamics of the life which Jesus led.

This approach attempts to build habits of beholding the world with a contemplative heart such that contemplative bonding takes place as the person moves through daily life.

Such habits take time to build, but they do indeed seem possible and fit the criteria described previously.

The simplest place to begin is with the physical world around us where God's creative hand is at work in wondrous ways. Even in an urban world where adult hearts grow jaded a renewed contemplative habit, so like the wonder of children, can be rebuilt to view the earth with our hearts and to find beauty and wonder.

A second area of living provides a rich core for building contemplative habits in daily life. This prayer seems to have been most basic to Jesus and may even be said to be the prayer of God—contemplating people. Habits can be built by which we accustom ourselves regularly to "see" other people, whether in direct encounters or even in passing, in a way of openness of heart which makes the growth of relationships possible.

This habit of contemplating people, when vigorous, brings fresh discoveries not only of new people who might pass unnoticed, but between people whose love reaches back through decades of familiarity.

Contemplating God is central to the core of our faith, whether the experience be direct and approaching mystical prayer, or whether we journey the ordinary pilgrim's path of following the Jesus of the Scriptures while we encounter the Spirit of Jesus in our hearts, our private praying, in the Eucharist and in the events of our daily living.

If our love for ourselves is to be the measure of our love for our neighbor, then contemplating ourselves with love is an integral dimension of life in the great commandment. Such contemplation can pass beyond the microscope of endless self-analysis to behold and to accept the person whom God has placed upon the earth to share the work of salvation.

'Noisy contemplation' enters powerfully into our struggles to love deeply and to summon forth justice upon the earth. The very contemplation of the tensions and conflicts can offer a way to integrate the fragmentation and heal the draining sense of "burn-out" with which people in extended struggles so often must cope. When all else failed, it was in contemplative praying over His deep struggles that Jesus, in the Garden, found the wholeness to go forward with his ministry, no matter what the cost.

The imaginative power of contemplation to reach out and establish caring and commitment across thousands of miles makes it the primary means for societal bonding. Passing beyond information and knowledge, contemplation can let us enter into the experiences and struggles of our sisters and brothers across the globe, to establish ties and commitment of heart.

Such contemplative bonding links strongly with the mission sense of such contemplatives as Thérèse of Lisieux and Thomas Merton, as well as with the simple but powerful way in which early generations of Catholics "ransomed pagan babies," and gave them a name.

MONSIGNOR ROMERO: THE FINAL MINISTRY

7. *The final ministry of Monsignor Romero provides signs of the development of such a spirituality.*

I began with a brief summary of the closing years of the life and ministry of Monsignor Romero. I would now like to focus on his life in light of the previous reflections.

The Earlier Years

Romero was a solitary person throughout his life. He was a prayerful person, as all witnesses testify, often going apart to pray.

His lifestyle was that of an ordinary "cleric" of his day, especially one trained in Rome who served the church in a largely institutional way, attended to its inner needs and, in that ministry, found his own way in faith.

The institutional church rewarded him with appropriate advancement until he was appointed Archbishop of San Salvador, the capital of El Salvador.

Although the Second Vatican Council had been over for almost twelve years when Romero became Archbishop in 1977, and although the Latin American bishops' meeting had taken place nine years previously in Medellin, neither seems to have profoundly impacted on his life or ministry.

One collaborator said of his prior ministry as Bishop of Santiago de Maria, an area of coffee-growing highlands and cotton-growing coastal plains:

> At that time Romero believed that the church was made up of the "good rich" and the "good poor," and he put as much distance as possible between himself and the "bad rich" and the revolutionary poor.[1]

Romero entered his final ministry still committed to a vision of the great commandment as deeply oriented to the transcendent God, a journey of each Christian seeking personal salvation, an essentially individualistic journey.

Romero appears to have undergone a contemplative awakening from the events which occurred at the beginning of his episcopacy. The events surrounding the post-election massacre at Plaza Libertad and the assassination of Rutilio Grande began a powerful process of change.

In company with many other people he began to look at and listen to (i.e., to contemplate) the Salvadoran reality. He encouraged people to bring him their stories of suffering and pain. He had to confront the persecution that broke out against the church as it moved to ally itself with the poor.

Romero's life and style of ministry began to make some striking changes.

a. *He began to work with the people in dialogue.*

Where previously he had been the typical bishop who made decisions himself, Romero began to consult widely with people from the young to the old, farmworker, university people, labor union workers, et cetera.

Romero began to welcome and to encourage collaboration among priests, religious and lay people. He himself began to collaborate with people whom he had formerly held in suspicion. Romero later confided that, when appointed Archbishop, he had accepted the task of reining in the 'subversive' priests and the base communities of the poor. They became among his closest collaborators.

Romero converted a chancery room to a 'coffee lounge,' and the place became a center where people from every walk of life gathered and shared news, hopes and tragedies.

Cooperation and dialogue as equals among members of the church replaced separation and "hierarchy" among priests, religious and lay people.

b. *Romero committed the church to the poor and took on their concerns.*

Where previously he had tried to steer a path between 'good rich' and 'good poor' and the 'bad rich' and the revolutionary poor, he now made a fundamental option for the poor and committed the church to their needs.

The journey was in no sense an easy one for him. He struggled with the implications of violence, and was deeply challenged over the question of violence and revolution. He went through periods of pulling back from collaborators, and had to struggle with conflict and mistrust among co-workers.

Conflict and tension became his constant companions. Persecution broke out against the church. He faced powerful ideological splits with his brother bishops.

With this suffering a shift of priorities took place in the lifestyle of the institutional church of San Salvador. The church's focus moved from a primary concern with preservation of the institutional church to focus on the concrete reality of the people's present existence. As Romero said:

> I am a shepherd who, with his people, has begun to learn a beautiful and difficult truth: our Christian faith requires that we submerge ourselves in this world.
>
> The course taken by the church has always had political repercussions. The problem is how to direct that influence so that it will be in accordance with the faith.
>
> The world that the church must serve is the world of the poor, and the poor are the ones who decide what it means for the church to really live in the world. [2]

Legalities of intra-church life were muted in the face of survival needs. Liturgy and Eucharist moved out of the churches and into the gatherings of the people, often clandestinely in their homes, or publicly, at demonstrations.

c. *Romero repeatedly spoke out against the injustices done to the poor.*

Not only did Monsignor Romero affirm the poor, but he denounced the injustices and the people who perpetuated them.

With the help of many people, his Sunday homilies, his pastoral letters and his regular broadcasts over the diocesan radio station

YSAX, became the voice for the poor of El Salvador and the most listened-to programs in El Salvador.

Not even the regular bombings of the radio station could stifle his voice. Church people gathered the resources to repair the station or made imaginative hook-ups by telephone to stations which broadcast from neighboring countries.

This bishop of reported caution and supposedly fragile health, in dialogue with the community, had grown bold and vigorous in sharing the story of the people.

d. *Together with many others Romero analyzed events in El Salvador. He identified the sources of evil and suffering, and denounced the injustices done to the people.*

Sometimes the denunciations were general:

> The church has committed itself to the world of the poor . . . The words of the prophets of Israel still hold true for us: there are those who would sell a just person for money and a poor person for a pair of sandals. There are those who fill their houses with violence, fill their houses with what they have stolen. There are those who crush the poor . . . while lying on beds of the most exquisite marble. There are those who take over house after house, field after field until they own the whole territory and are the only ones in it.[3]

Sometimes he spoke specifically:

> The cause of the evil here is the oligarchy, a small nucleus of families who don't care about the hunger of the people . . . I have warned the oligarchy time and again to open their hands, give away their fancy rings because if they don't the time will come when they will be cut off . . . The present government totally lacks popular support and is kept in power only by the armed forces and the support of foreign powers. The Christian Democratic presence in the junta functions only to disguise the repressive character of the present regime, especially outside the country.[4]

e. *Romero, even when he spoke of political events, sought to follow the Gospel.*

In February 1980 he repeated a tireless theme:

> If by the necessity of the moment I am throwing light on the politics of our land, I do so only as a pastor, shedding the light of the gospel . . . We are not politicians who confide in merely human strength. We are, above all, Christians, and we know that if God does not build our civilization, the builders build in vain. That is why we know that our strength comes from prayer and conversion to God.[5]

f. *Romero, even as he sensed death drawing close, continued to speak boldly.*

Toward the end, Romero, the recipient of repeated death threats, sensed that death was drawing near. He refused protection, "The shepherd does not want security as long as the flock does not have security."[6]

His final days contained some of his boldest, most direct preaching. His letter to President Carter, deploring the sending of United States military and economic aid, has already been mentioned, and the escalating violence it predicted would be the result of United States involvement has been tragically verified with forty thousand deaths.

His final plea to the soldiers appears to have sealed his death:

> I would like to issue a special entreaty to the members of the army, and specifically to the ranks of the National Guard, the police and the military. Brothers and sisters, you are our own people; you kill your fellow peasants. Someone's order to kill should not prevail; rather, what ought to prevail is the law of God that says, "Do not kill." No soldier is obliged to obey an order against the law of God; no one has to fulfill an immoral law. There is still time for you to follow your conscience, even in the face of a sinful order to kill.[7]

On the following day he was assassinated as he celebrated the Eucharist, dying with Christ's words of forgiveness on his lips.

The Impact of Romero's Ministry

As long as the Salvadoran church was perceived as an institution which led its own life and stayed in its own domain, civil leaders and the oligarchy of families in this "Catholic" country could deal with it. When it became a church of the people, taking up their hopes and joys, their sufferings and their sorrows, it was perceived as a church dealing with the same problems as the ruling class and thus viewed as a competitor. It was quickly and rightly labelled "subversive."

The subversion was not "communist," as claimed, but the power of the Good News.

Just as Jesus had to be eliminated when his ministry among the people appeared to gain a following and to change the way in which people perceived their rights, duties and destiny, i.e., a challenge to the status quo, so Romero and the style of ministry he represented had to be eliminated when it encouraged the people, especially the poor, to change the way in which they perceived their existence.

Building upon the work of the "communidades de base" and their affirmation of people as beloved sons and daughters of God, worthy of deep respect, Romero affirmed the poor, praised their organizations, denounced the violence done to keep them in their historically subservient social position, encouraged them to take responsibility for their own existence. Yet, he challenged them not to use violent means unless all other means were denied them. He pledged that the church would accompany them on their journey and minister to them in their struggle.

It is no wonder that Romero became the sort of threat that Jesus represented, and met the same fate.

As one Salvadoran described his impact, "When Mnsgr Romero became a bishop, the church of San Salvador was an institution, a place for the rich. When he died, it had become the church of the people."[8]

CONCLUSION

In broad strokes, I have tried to advance the belief that Christians in general are being called to look at the great commandment in a new way. This path reflects the fourfold way we experience God's Spirit in our lives, i.e., directly in loving communion with God, and in the experience of bonding in love and solidarity with ourselves and with sisters and brothers near and far who are our neighbors.

This path of life in the great commandment demands an expansion of our spirituality and our concepts of prayer to support people who live busy, active lives involved in ministry and the struggle to build a more just world. The very experiences of our living can become, as they were for Jesus, a source of nourishment and contemplative bonding.

After describing some discernment signs for such a spirituality, I described the emergence of such a spirituality in the closing years of Archbishop Romero's life and ministry, as he began to "accompany the people" on their journey.

His journey took on the characteristics of Jesus' ministry and reaped the suffering reward that Jesus promised. In the hearts and lives of many Christians, Romero continues to witness the resurrection which Jesus proclaimed would come to all who follow after him in love and solidarity.

NOTES

[1] Placido Erdozain, *Archbishop Romero* (Maryknoll, New York: Orbis Books, 1981).
[2] Speech at Louvain University, 2 February 1980.
[3] *Ibid.*
[4] Homily, 23 March 1980.
[5] Homily, 17 February 1980.
[6] Homily, 22 July 1979.
[7] Homily, 23 March 1980.
[8] Personal communication, Anonymous.

Index of Persons